ARK

INNER WORK IN THE WOUNDED AND CREATIVE

David Roomy began his studies of Jungian psychology in 1963 with M. Esther Harding and William H. Kennedy, then president of the C. G. Jung Foundation of New York. He later taught Jungian psychology at Friends World College in New York and in England and was lecturer in Psychology at the British Campus of New England College. He was certified as a qualified practitioner of the form of therapy he utilizes by Arnold Mindell, founder of the Research Society for Process Oriented Psychology in Zurich, Switzerland. He is in private practice in Vancouver, British Columbia, Canada, and travels widely, offering workshops in this field. As a clinical supervisor in a psychiatric institution, he had personal contact with over 1,000 clients during an eight-year period.

INNER WORK
IN THE WOUNDED
AND CREATIVE

·

The Dream in the Body

DAVID ROOMY

ARKANA

ARKANA

Published by the Penguin Group
27 Wrights Lane, London W8 5TZ, England
Viking Penguin Inc., 40 West 23rd Street, New York, New York 10010, USA
Penguin Books Australia Ltd, Ringwood, Victoria, Australia
Penguin Books Canada Ltd, 2801 John Street, Markham, Ontario, Canada L3R 1B4
Penguin Books (NZ) Ltd, 182–190 Wairau Road, Auckland 10, New Zealand

Penguin Books Ltd, Registered Offices: Harmondsworth, Middlesex, England.

First published 1990
1 3 5 7 9 10 8 6 4 2

Filmset in 10 on 12pt Baskerville
Made and printed in Great Britain by
Cox & Wyman Ltd, Reading

For the thousands of psychiatric patients
for whom there may still be a key
to the powers within

A disease may be its own healing process.

Arnold Mindell

The Sea is the body; the two Fishes are the Spirit and the Soul.

From a manuscript of 'The Book of Lambspring'

Contents

Acknowledgment

Without my discovery of Arnold Mindell and his process-oriented psychology, this work would never have come into being.

Introduction

Process-oriented psychology convinces many who experience it that there is some deeper process behind the problems of life. When this deeper process is carefully related to, then a larger Self may come into awareness. The experience is often so powerful that it has the capacity to motivate one to continue working with the physio-psychological processes that are attempting to enlarge the awareness and experience of one's life. Would this approach be effective with those relegated to mental institutions? That was the question I first began to explore when I started to use process-oriented psychology with people who were regarded as chronically mentally ill.

I did not know what the outcome of the attempt would be. Some five years after the beginning of my study of the use of this method I had data indicating that the method is, indeed, effective. Not only that: I had an appreciation and experience of psychological processes that of their very nature appear to be conditions, even intransigent conditions, but, when worked with, may become wider possibilities for the human personality.

I was not unaffected by these discoveries. I think of myself at the beginning as being guided by a conception: to test the effectiveness of a methodology. It was as if I began with a concept, as Pope Julius did when he originally presented to Michelangelo his idea for covering the ceiling of the Sistine Chapel. But what emerged, as creative process unfolded, was infinitely beautiful and charged. Process is the organizing principle behind human experience, both psychological and physiological. It will be part of my purpose to share what I have found: something beautiful and purposeful in the otherwise dark and vacant caverns of patients' minds. To see some transformation in this dark material is something that would touch almost every heart.

Delightful as the six clients are whose stories are told here, it would perhaps be a limitation of a good, overall story not also to look elsewhere than among extreme forms of mental disorder. Therefore I have included here another kind of drama. It is about the expansion of four growth-oriented people on a journey to Greece. Theirs is the dance of process as it interacts with, and transforms, the ways in which the conditions of life are experienced, through which, at the end, one is able to say yes to life and to live it.

Ironically, the areas of creativity and spirituality reflected in the four architects and in Chad and Antoine, whom we will meet later, are sometimes the most deeply suspect in the eyes of those who work in mental institutions. However, creative and spiritual people are very aware of imbalanced situations in the world and in themselves and seek to create a new balance within themselves at the very least. By exploring their processes we may see processes that compensate for the more one-sided forces that are dominant in the world. Also the way in which these people work with processes may be of some relevance to more unbalanced people, like those who are experiencing psychosis. What is needed is awareness. Process work, with its discovery of awareness in seldom accessed aspects of human experience and information in the body, may provide an important new approach.

Process-oriented psychology does not limit itself to work with individual problems. It attempts to work with the global aspects of the person, including physical and relationship problems, group experiences and conflict resolution in larger units of societies.

The world as it exists may not be in a very good position to work with psychotic people. It is from this world that many psychotic people flee. Indeed, there is a crisis in the psychiatric world itself, described by one psychiatrist in this way: she says that on the one hand there is almost total reliance on neuroleptic medications in the treatment of people with psychotic disorders and, on the other hand, despair about working with these people in any other way. This is reflected in the fact that very little is being written about psychotherapy for extremely unbalanced people.

Although seemingly depressed, rejected as unworkable, relegated to a treadmill of repetitive behavior and stuck with
unchanging symbols, mental patients can find the psychic life
behind their illness, and the great pattern of the human being is
able to unfold itself again in them. That's what is beautiful.

Since I started writing this book I have discovered much more
about the theme through working with people outside a residential facility, some of whom were experiencing hallucinations. One
person, through support and a gradual shifting of channels from
vision to movement, was able to discover her own strength and
go on with her life rather than balancing on the edge of suicide.
Another person, again through the support of a group, was able
to sleep again, without being awakened by terrifying dreams,
and to work through a process that had been debilitating to her.

Well-meaning people may conclude that these two people
should have been hospitalized for their own safety, but that
expedient could have been just the beginning of stories of
institutionalized people such as those I shall recount. The point
of process work is that any process can be worked through, even
a psychotic one.

It is in the nature of processes that they seem at first to be
unresolvable states: the person is identified only with what
appears to be happening. No matter what *appears* to be happening, there is always something else that is happening. It is
discovered through a signal, something the person is doing, in
addition to what he or she is saying. That signal is the key to the
vital secondary process. Following such signals and switches, as
well as understanding the structure of primary and secondary
process, is what process work is about.

The lives of Chad and Antoine, and those of the four architects,
that comprise Part Three present the poetry and beauty of inner
experience. They are meant to show the essence and flowering of
creative inner work.

PART ONE

·

Heritage and Methodology

1 • Process-oriented Psychology and the Spiritual Tradition

I would like you to share the experience of process-oriented psychology. I would like you to understand how it manifests itself. What attracted me to this field were the discernible signs of its success as a method for working with people's processes and the compassion I experienced at the hands of its founder, Arnold Mindell.

In the cases cited here you will observe how the signatures of the psyche/body express themselves, the information they impart. We are consciously aware of only part of the information. What is not known is of immense value: it is like a stone rejected by builders that may become the chief cornerstone of the building. It is as if conscious life strives to turn from recognition. The psyche/body processes try to right the often tilted vessel of conscious life through messages from the other side.

There is an established discipline to process-oriented psychology that, as it were, makes accessible information that has remained largely hidden from the individual or group; therefore my plan here will be to discuss the thought patterns of energetic life, so that you begin to get an awareness of how they are manifested.

In process-oriented psychology there is a profound trust in working with what comes. The preparation for the process worker lies in learning to be open, learning to follow signals from a therapeutic session, such as the tapping of a foot, a rush of color to the cheeks and so on. It involves a profound trust expressed in a concrete moment with a specific individual, a trust of that person's particularity, humanity, process – however strange, uncharted, incomparable.

One theme of this book is rebirth. Jung's sense of this is the restoration of an original oneness with the Self. This oneness may have been expressed at some time in this life, and may exist in one's recollection, or it may belong to another lifetime.

In dreambody experiences the deeper Self is addressed, that totality of expression and experience that goes beyond the concerns of everyday life. Jung believed the Self to lie in the body, a view that perhaps contrasts with many of the teachings we have received. And to some of us our bodies may not be places of easy access.

The deep can seem frightening. We grasp the here and now sometimes in terror. Process work allows whatever process is active in oneself to find expression.

Process work follows channels of information, the ways in which information comes to us, visually or aurally, through body feelings or motion. It focuses both on processes that are known and on those that are more or less unknown. It follows switches of channels as a person changes, let us say, from talking to feeling something in his or her body. It recognizes edges, the inhibition felt about confronting information that is not completely known.

Process-oriented psychology looks at the fabric, the intersecting energies, of one's dreambody and regards body symptoms, dreams and relationship problems as having to do with a subtle but ever-present reality.

Process work seeks awareness. It is not interested in cheap tricks. When awareness comes, through a therapeutic session or through working on oneself alone, then there is a new overall consciousness with which to regard concrete problems. It is as if the problems shift and are no longer inscrutable. The new knowledge about oneself opens up a way where sunlight floods perception and herculean effort is no longer necessary.

Process work respects the individual and whatever is happening in a person, however unusual. This work, whether undertaken by process worker and client or shared by a group of people, respects the protective container of confidentiality.

'Our hearts are restless until they find their rest in thee': so has written the great St Augustine. Jung has written that as long as the God-image in a human being is not being related to, that life cannot be complete. The God-image, which Jung has called the Self, is the essence of completing what Jung called 'wholeness'. Presumably it contains all parts of the psyche, all parts of human make-up. Although Jung has said that Christ is an image of the Self, we should not fasten on to that one image because in any one person's life this particular image of the Self may not come up. Jung writes in his autobiography about a dream (see page 93); in the dream, he recounts, he entered a profound experience signalled by an open chapel door, and on the altar, where he might have expected to find an image of Christ or the Virgin, he found instead simply a radial flower.

In Nafplion, Greece, recently I was studying the designs on pottery found at Mycenae and Tiryns and other Minoan and pre-Minoan sites dating from 2400 BC. The designs were forms of the *maiandros* (labyrinthine pattern), which leads the eye inwards and then outward again, into and out of the maze just as Ariadne so dramatically enabled Theseus to find his way into and out of the maze in Greek myth. There were also designs of waves and flowers. On a great burial urn there were simple, undulating lines.

I cannot express how satisfying it was to me to see these patterns. It felt as if the human psyche that was present there all those millennia ago was the same as my own, that we breathed the same spiritual/bodily air of life. If the psyche was so old, and was recognized in its true age by me, then it would go on, and the particular concerns of my life were not very important beside this spiritual truth. But to live that way, with the vitality, faith and forwardness of energy expressed in those designs by early Greeks, to integrate this God-image, to bring it close – that was my hope. To live each day, each moment, as if that image of original unity, oneness with the wholeness of bodily/psychological reality, that transpersonal quality of human life, were present in me! The Hindu greeting *namasta* salutes the God in the person whom one meets. The Quaker philosopher George Fox spoke of 'that of God in every person'. Process work is about acquiring a relationship with the deeper Self that may motivate our life and existence. If that Self does not motivate our existence, we may not be so keen on living.

Process work has some terminology for this. Let us return to

Jung's view of the God-image as completeness. It follows that this image contains contrasts, opposites – for example, reason and passion, spirit and body, love and aggression, depression and elation, hope and despair, nighttime and daytime consciousness, Sun and Moon, male and female. It belongs to life to incorporate these extremes, just as the Taoist philosopher might.

But, alas, we are conditioned to identify with one side or the other. Some people are more given to order, to this-wordly concerns. It is especially characteristic of this age that the God-image, as Martin Buber has characterized it, is 'eclipsed'. One sees many people living as if there were no spiritual reality – perhaps in opposition to it, perhaps in terror, perhaps resentful at having it forced down their throats by well-meaning (and maybe by some less disinterested) religious people.

For some sexuality is also repressed, though in the case of the Greek vases it is frankly there. Jung has stated that much of Western theology is a development of the thinking (as opposed to feeling) function. He characterizes Islam, by contrast, as a religion molded around Eros. The integration of contrasts is a move towards wholeness.

In process work we recognize that there is generally an identification with one part or many. What I identify with is called my *primary process*; what is not so clearly acknowledged, often opposite in nature, is the *secondary process*.

Our work is to use process psychology and methods as we greet what emerges in the work. No particular quality needs be implied. For a saint to discover his dirty feet might be a revelation. Although the God-image sounds rather grand, it would be misleading to see process work as identified with any image. Seriousness is balanced by play. What comes up is the guide. No judgments, no expectations – simply following what emerges for any particular individual is the way of process-oriented psychology. I trust that whatever you may need at this time is there, and that will be right.

There is a wonderful Hasidic story. A man left on a journey because he dreamed of buried gold. He left his family and traveled far. His journey continued for many years, and when he was passing through yet another city he found his shoes, which he had left out during the night, turned around. And he realized it was his own home. He dug in the back yard there and found the gold.

It is natural to strive after union with God, the watercourse way, Buddha, enlightenment, the soul, the inner gold, Jahweh, Asclepius. There are several cautions, however. Those great mystics who lived with God had first to build their houses strong. A friend of mine used to say that before you can sacrifice the ego, you must establish it. The Buddhists talk about absolute and relative truth: the two are never separate. It is true both that we are energy and emptiness, and that our children's hugs around our knees are real. We participate in both the spirit and the body. What is most profound is also most simple. 'Our hearts are restless until they find their rest in Thee.'

All spiritual truth has to do with balance. This is a very comforting thought. We do not need to leave behind our nature. In the Taoist way nature is our true guide. Suzuki, the great teacher, commented upon religious views that put God against man, God against nature, man against nature. It does not make any sense, he poignantly reflects.

Another caution warns against clinging. For the Buddhists clinging is the cause of mental confusion. A person may say, 'I had this great vision, this wonderful dream. A certain spirit appeared to me. Now I can justify my life, my suffering.' In process work we take what is happening. If suffering comes today, I don't have to cling to my vision of yesterday or last year. By the Tibetan Book of the Dead we are urged to be prepared to see both the peaceful and the wrathful deities of the *bardo* as the thought forms in our own minds.

In the Roman Catholic Church, among followers of the mystic tradition, what leads from mystical experience is the service to the widow and orphan. This leads us to the bonding with others and our need for them in order to complete our vision. There are many terms for this: the fellowship of Christians, the Buddhist *Sanga*, the Jung club, the world of relationship for process people. A Christian priest notes that the Lord's Prayer begins 'Our Father', not 'My Father'. A Buddhist nun offers the following formula: call on the highest spirits. Ask them to come. Don't go for anything less. Let these be the sources of our motivation. When they have come, dedicate the moment, and their presence in it, to the liberation of all sentient beings.

The Christian leader whom I have already mentioned told me of Pope John XXIII's vision that Christ was simply one revelation of God, that God was the bigger, the unknown, and that in Him Christians meet people of other faiths and views. None of us knows what Jung's 'greatest intensity', unextended intensity, is precisely. To perceive even part of this we need all the other parts, which other people in our communities can give us.

Finally, there is a vision and a methodology in process work that aims at the realization of wholeness in relationships, small groups, larger groups, nations and, finally, the globe itself. Process work is dedicated to bringing about that realization of wholeness, awareness, because through it we can hope for resolution of conflict.

What we have is a great gift. Process work says, 'What you are doing is right.' Where we are already serving, giving, we are worshipping, in an informal way, the archetypes, the spirits and beings of nature and the inner world. How important what we are already doing is to the world! A priest sees work with people, such as will be described in this book, as an informal liturgy. In the great ocean is an island. As consciousness comes, more islands emerge and reach out to each other.

Jung's vision was that human beings getting to know the world and themselves consciously are the consciousness of the world.

2 • *Dreambody Work: the Foundation, the Method and the Clients*

Jungian Psychology, Dreamwork and Psychosis

During the course of this book I have not dwelt on interpretations, such as an analysis of the theme of messianism in Albert's work (Chapter 6), which would be possible in the light of the rich fund of symbols available in Jungian or analytical psychology. Material from the collective unconscious is important to therapists and to their training, yet process-oriented psychology does not dwell on interpretations; it moves with a process.

In Albert's case a new person unfolded before my eyes. At the end changes occurred almost daily. Although the theme of messianism was always present, I didn't think that he needed to be confronted with it intellectually, as some therapy schools would advocate. I stuck with the process, trusting our capacity to talk about anything and everything, and with the daily evolution that was apparent in Albert. By asking a particular question I got an individual response; Albert's image of the Messiah was the 'cutting edge'. If he was able to get his life in order, in some way he might be able to realize that 'cutting edge'.

I told him at one point that when people can identify with one of these larger-than-life figures, the archetypes, their lives are less isolated. An individual may have a sense of giftedness, but loss of humanity may be the consequence. Neil Michlem, a psychiatrist and Jungian analyst, describes this in an article on hysteria. He writes, speaking of a client's dream:

This is reminiscent of a paradoxical statement of Jung's in discussing how relative are the states of consciousness and unconsciousness. He says 'there is a consciousness in which unconsciousness predominates,

9

as well as consciousness in which self-consciousness predominates.'
The dream describes what can be a gifted, almost privileged, state of
one living so close to those reservoirs of all the dark psyche has to offer.
It is, however, cursed by the lack of stability with which to confront the
dangers as well as the values within this reservoir.[1]

Treatment, as it exists today, is not simply a matter of gaining
awareness, and process-oriented psychology is altogether a newcomer. Since the 1960s the treatment of choice for people with
psychotic disorders has been psychotropic medication with
phenothiazines. I believe that such medication simply closes off
the psyche. A friend of mine, a physician, has written a paper on
tardive dyskinesia, the largely irreversible disorder that is the
consequence of prolonged use of such medication. Dr Pautler has
provided an extract of some of his points. I quote:

> Tardive dyskinesia is a result of a hypersensitivity of dopamine
> adrenergic receptors that follows long-term blocking of these recep-
> tors by phenothiazine drugs. In other words, you might say that the
> receptors themselves are now hyperactive, and this hyperactivity
> results in the movement disorder known as tardive dyskinesia. Now,
> both Parkinsonism and tardive dyskinesia are movement disorders,
> but very different in their appearance. Parkinsonism results from
> direct blocking of the dopamine adrenergic receptors and there is
> rigidity, slowness to initiate motion, pill-rolling tremor, etc. Tardive
> dyskinesia, as mentioned above, is caused by the hyperactivity or
> hypersensitivity of the dopamine adrenergic receptors and is a much
> more violent movement disorder than seen with Parkinson's disease.
> As you know, you see jerks, bizarre grimacing, frog-like tongue
> thrusting, etc. . . . In the case of tardive dyskinesia, you could say
> that the body is paying a price for the repression of psychoses. I think
> there is something in saying that the psychoses may, with the use of
> these medications, drop into body and be expressed this way.[2]

When you have seen over a thousand clients who are being
treated by psychiatrists with such psychotropic medications, and
have observed the effects on body movements, you have to
suspect atrophy of personality and intelligence as well and ask
yourself if there isn't something more.

True, psychotropic medications emptied the mental hospitals

in the 1960s and early 1970s. But at what price? Believe me, if you had a relative who, you were told, had to be treated with medications that would have such effects after their prolonged use, you would want to think twice, because that relative would look quite different at the end of the day. However, you would probably be told that there was no alternative.

This was one of the reasons why I, as a psychotherapist working in an institution for those being treated with phenothiazines by psychiatrists, began searching for another method.

All the clients presented in the early chapters of this book were on medications and were seen regularly by a psychiatrist while I was working with them. Michlem speaks of medication's 'undeniable therapeutic contribution toward enhancing psychic accessibility'.[3] As Michlem states, psychosis is a process, viewed mythically, that leads to a terrible place, to an image that is intolerable to consciousness, an image that can break the walls of consciousness.

One doesn't get to that image quickly. When the time arrives in the process for that image to emerge in a person, it is a scary moment. Will the client again be catapulted to the far ends of the earth? One must be able to judge then whether to go on. In some of our clients the process argued for going on. Trust, and a lot of support, were essential. Arnold Mindell is quite clear that *this method should not be applied without specific training*. In *City Shadows* Mindell develops his approach with people who were regarded as having psychotic disorders. He shows, with apparent ease and consummate skill, that the secondary process of such people can be worked with. His point is that the psychosis has become the primary process, the one with which the person identifies.

Speaking of Jung's definition of the Self, Michael Fordham writes, 'The self is the totality that unites opposites, and is thus a synthesis of all psychic elements . . . Jung by implication refers to the self as bodily and indeed once asserted that the self – meaning its symbolic representation – grew out of the body . . .'[4] This is the nature of process-oriented psychology, or dreambody work; it is to bring in the Self. It can start anywhere, perhaps with a physical symptom such as headaches. It can work with anyone – Mindell has addressed his work to 'extreme states' such as terminal illnesses and psychosis.

This book is meant to be a companion piece to *City Shadows* and to show that a real impact is made on the overall condition of people receiving treatment through process-oriented psychology if their condition is followed over a course of time. It is meant to answer a question that evolves naturally from a reading of Mindell's brilliant study of dealing with the first few sentences of the client. The question is: what about follow-up? The follow-up here has been with clients suffering from a condition referred to as 'chronic'. I don't like the term; it implies a condition that is not going to change. 'Process' (derived from process-oriented psychology) suggests change and all that this implies.

The Method

What is the method? I will not go into great detail but would prefer to allow you to experience the method through these four people as it worked for them.

Body is important. There are body signals or experiences around which the work turns. But body does not convey all because it is as if behind body are patterns, basic images that, once they have emerged, continue to unfold. And that's why we call this process. Process is an inner image unfolding into its fullness or completeness.

To speak of process you have to talk about the individual because that's the only package this experience comes in. Process is, by definition, individual: it happens in a particular person; its form is individual. To meet people as if one knew what to expect – or, worse, what to give – is a violation of process. Process begins to unfold when the secondary process is entered into; an unoccupied channel is manifest; a symptom or involuntary, unwary gesture is amplified; or new experiences occur on their own.

Any new terminology seems like jargon until the definitions are fleshed out by experiencing them in action. Let's start with definitions.

Primary process is what you identify with. I am a law-abiding engineer from Minnesota, with a grandmother from Fiji, and I always get the job done. My *secondary process* is usually the opposite. To continue with this example, whereas I go to all the reunions for people from Minnesota now living in northern New Mexico, I really have some poor memories of my 'favorite' state. And although I am an engineer, I really harbor thoughts of being an artist. Although we are proud of my grandmother, she was very cruel. Finally, I have been told that I stretch the law. Thus we can paint a picture of the secondary process. It is the opposite of the primary. This basic concept, as it applies to psychosis, is formulated in *City Shadows*.[5]

Channels are ways of apprehending and treating information. There is a group of channels: visual, auditory, kinesthetic, proprioceptive, relationship and world. 'I see,' you may say. This places your current apprehending in the *visual channel*; something I have written has caused you to visualize something that you 'see'. You will probably be able to verbalize easily about this channel. The visual channel uses the eyes. It also apprehends through inner images. Sometimes outer experiences coincide with inner images.

The *auditory channel* pertains to perception and apperception on the basis of sound. A musician friend once explained to me that light doesn't have rhythm. And although hologram theory has broadened our appreciation of the subject of light waves, from a practical point of view my friend is right. The channel of hearing is much more vital to him personally. The same holds true culturally. 'Hear, O Israel . . .' Those ancient words hark back to an identity of a people based upon hearing, upon words and sounds.

When we leave these two channels we depart from territory familiar to most of us. I am speaking now of the *kinesthetic* and the *proprioceptive* channels. Movement or kinesthesis is the main channel of dancers and dance therapists. They apprehend objects, events, relationships and space through kinesthesis. A whole different world lies there.

Proprioception concerns the experience of gravity and the position of the limbs and torso by the joints, muscles and skeleton

13

of the body. Posture is a key term of this channel. A slouch is an expressive experience of weight. Ask someone who has spent three days crumpled in a small box, as a friend of mine once did during a bombing attack in Vietnam,[6] about proprioception.

The *relationship channel* concerns working things out between oneself and others. It is very important for me to let you know how I feel about what you did – a typical relationship approach. It will be observed that some people's need for relationship is greater than others'. Martin Buber was one of the great exponents of this channel. Reality lies 'in between' I and thou.[7]

The *world channel* is active in those who have a keen perception of nature, for example. Stepping off a small boat on an uninhabited island, an acquaintance of mine was taken with finding eagle feathers floating on the waves at the shore. Here the world channel was in the forefront. The world channel may involve a religious experience of nature. Introverted people over thirty years old sometimes suddenly become interested in the world; they are occupying their world channel, according to Mindell.[8]

In the set of basic concepts important to process-oriented psychology we come next to *amplification*. Amplification in this context simply means to make a body signal stronger. That body signal may be a gesture – something that is being expressed with the hands while a person is talking about a problem, for example. Here we encounter the intersection of the channels. While the person is describing in words an inability to meet deadlines, for example, his or her hands may be flailing the air. Although the person may be slightly aware that his or her hands are moving, the hand motions are largely unconscious by comparison with the verbal description. We can say the hand motions represent a channel that is less 'occupied' – that is, less awareness and facility exist there than in the occupied verbal/auditory channel.

There are two basic ways of amplifying. A therapist can simply say to the person, 'Could you make that stronger?' This is an act of active imagination with which the body usually complies. A second way is to provide slight resistance, which has the same effect as the client's voluntarily increasing the signal. In the case of the hand gestures described earlier, these could be resisted by the therapist using his own hand gently to impede the hand of the client as it makes its arc motion outward.

Amplification is important in the treatment of physical symptoms. There is a message behind what the body is doing. When a gesture or symptom is amplified, the dream behind it may come into awareness.

With those who have been impaired through long-term confinement there sometimes seems to be missing the spark that is present in others and may involve others more actively in their own treatment initially. It is sometimes the case with the chronically mentally ill that the therapist has to represent physically the processes that are arising in a client's work. This may involve, for example, the therapist doing some of the role playing for the client until he or she regains some of the outer energy and confidence that are necessary in order for the client to take a more active role in his or her own therapeutic processes.

It is not recommended that you try these approaches without training. But this small excursion into theory has been necessary to provide a road map for the discussion of the work that follows. As Mindell states: 'One's important experiences come through that person's unoccupied channels.' Incursion into the secondary process is revitalizing, quickening – in the language of dreambody, it is the meeting of Mercurius. The integration of the secondary process is like Jung's concept of the transcendent function and Hegel's synthesis after thesis and antithesis.

New experiences emerge when the patterns present in the secondary process and unoccupied channels are provided with a new way in which to unfold. These new experiences change the way in which energy flows and life is experienced thereafter.

Certain memories, vivid experiences and dream-like body states are linked with certain channels; these, when related to through the methods of process-oriented psychology, evoke patterns of experience that raise further speculation, research and questions. Although there are implications for information theory, physiological psychology, brain research and hologram theory, it is not our purpose here to explain these areas, fascinating as they may be.

It is important to know that in some people certain channels, such as proprioception, lie farther below the surface of awareness than others, such as the visual and auditory channels, both of which are associated with intellectual and verbal processes.

I feel that it is important to mention again psyche and dreams. They are synonymous. With body they make up the unit: psyche/ body or 'dreambody'. This relationship may be formulated in many different ways. For example, Mindell has mentioned that physical symptoms are processes trying to dream themselves into existence. Process is a fluid way of regarding a pattern. At the same time, working with the body that acknowledges all the background to dreams or images, as developed by Jung, is a new way of evolvement and of therapy.

The experience of compassion features very strongly in process work. What is love? Perhaps another form of the question is needed. Is love so fundamental to human nature that it cannot be compared with anything else? Is it by nature also something more in movement, more living, than the word 'what' suggests? Where are we to look for a rendering of this lively form?

Love, or compassion, comes whenever our present preoccupations are transcended by participating in a moment with another human being, his or her moment becoming our moment. Some people give over their lives, as far as is possible, to such experiences. For human beings are longing for just this attentiveness from others. But there is more. If the participating with another is also accompanied by understanding, then we have gone a step beyond. And if this understanding can recognize the structure of psychic processes, and can encourage those in disguise that are crying out for expression, then we have touched upon something fundamental. Hiding behind all external forms are the symbols or forms that give expression to human life. To recognize these forms when they appear in existence, to seize upon and encourage them, that is the art.

Introducing the Clients

How did I happen to meet my clients? Joy, Rose, Monie and Albert I met in most unusual circumstances. I was invited to work for a short time as a therapist employing process-oriented psychology in a big hospital in one of the large Midwestern states. I was told by the assistant administrator that they wanted something that would shake up some of the staff who had become too complacent, thinking that medication was the only answer and, worse, that mental illness, as they referred to it, was beyond the pale of rehabilitation.

Dreambody work was just the ticket. The intention that was farthest from the minds of the hospital administrators was the application of bodywork to psychotics. It was so unconventional that the project could fail – safely. Everyone knows that the one thing you must not do with people who have had serious breakdowns is to introduce an experience that may excite them, provoke more breakdowns and instability and lead, finally, to chaos and suicide. If I had known what I was getting into, if I had known that I would bring down such wrath upon my head, then ... I would still have done it. Each of the clients was worth it.

I can see smiles forming on their faces now, where each of them sits today, long after our work. Some are in places recognized by the world as OK, one in a place judged not OK. But then it is not always where people end up that is important. What they have to tell us along the way bodes well for the future.

Some of the people described here have not had the extended life circumstances of many people. In the case of some of them friends are limited to other patients in psychiatric facilities and group homes. Family relationships are often truncated. For many of the chronically mentally ill work experience ceases after a few attempts at doing such jobs as dishwashing at restaurants. All these factors lead to a condition of limited outer stimulus and restricted interaction with others and with the culture at large. Often their personalities are not very extended in scope. Their intensity is inward. As such, it is interesting, for it is an open road of unconscious and psychological processes. The processes and developments of inner life are thus visible in all the contours of a steady, psychological world. Therefore I would ask the reader to look here rather than to the usual personality development we expect in characters, real or fictional.

The scientists among you will want to know certain facts at the start. How long did I work with them? Joy for a couple of sessions and contact over two years; Rose for six months; Monie for a year and a half; Albert for a brief, burning four months; and Chad and Antoine for many years.

Ages and demographics: all of them were middle-aged; all seemed younger. None had an established job. Joy, although very warm, had been anemic as a result of a lifelong physical condition that had left her frail. Rose had three girls. Monie had been divorced after a wedding that had taken place in another institution. Albert was celibate. All were North American.

Their identities must remain hidden, but what is reported here is true to the bone.

PART TWO

·

Working with the Wounded

3 • Joy

Late one summer I was asked to talk to Joy, as she had again been on suicide watch. She sat in a chair, with her head tilted forward at the neck so that her eyes were staring down directly at the floor. Her back was also tilted forward, and she maintained no eye contact with myself or with the others present in the room, three members of staff. Joy stated that she didn't have any reason to live, that she had just about given up. She had a history of frequent and intense suicidal ideation and attempts. Her diagnosis was borderline personality disorder. The staff, it was reported to me, had also given up on her. She had been on suicide watch many times during the past few months, since she had been at the facility. Her relevant past was that she had used the emergency suicide hotline in her community nightly for long periods of time, and during a period of six weeks prior to her coming to the facility she had again called nightly. My contact with her was not regular.

In the session she stated that she was not sure that she could carry on. It became clear from a one-line declaration that when she stopped caring for people, everything went to the winds: she lost control; she became impulsive; she heard voices; and she seized razor blades. I kept echoing her words: when she no longer cared for people, all these other very negative things took place. I asked her to locate this caring, the kind she had expressed at one point for another staff member who was present in the room, in her body. She said that it was in her heart and not in her stomach. That was where she felt things – in her heart.

About two months later

Joy asked to speak with me. There had been a death at the facility. It had been caused by an overdose and affected many of the clients, including Joy. She said that she had had a dream during the night following this disturbing episode. In this dream someone, or several people, had died. I told her that this was in contrast to previous dreams, in which she had been suicidal. In those earlier dreams she herself had died or nearly died. Her tone and manner were different from those of previous periods when she had spoken of death, though she was upset and shaken. Nevertheless, I had a sense that she was coping. I watched her talk, and I noticed that her right foot was about one inch off the floor. She kept it there for a long time. I noticed that her left foot was curled, even twisted, under her. I asked her what the right foot felt like. She said that at times it was tingly, and it felt as if it were floating. The left foot felt as if it were upside down. I echoed these statements to her in relation to her current state of mind. She changed positions, and her feet now touched the floor but only with the toes or ball of the foot. I asked what this felt like, and she said, 'Unbalanced.' She seemed to be interested in this discussion. I linked it with a pivotal talk that we had had once, in which she had related to her body and to the fact that she had warmth in her heart. This was at a time in which she had nearly given up on living, and it was the one positive sign that we could discover. I associated these things with her body and with listening to what her body had to say to her.

She commented on her poor posture, something that had come up before in our sessions together. She stated that her body was really telling her to straighten up. This was in connection with her current feeling of being unsettled and listening to voices and thinking about suicide. She went on to say that she had on the door of her room a daily reminder to give it a try or give it all she's got.

Joy was always nice to be with. For anyone with lots of time to talk, she would have been a pleasant companion. Her delight was in offering you something she had made. She seemed to

22

bring into the room good feeling, lots of it, born of a good disposition and her affection for people.

A year after the beginning

Joy had no further episodes of suicide ideation during the next six months while she remained at the facility. After discharge she started cooking dishes for friends, staff and clients and brought gifts to people at the institution when she came to visit. She lived in a boarding facility and was part of a work-training program. Five months after discharge she reported that she should be hospitalized psychiatrically. She had cut her arm when angry with her boss. She took pains to say to me that she was not trying to commit suicide. She said that this would be her first (psychiatric) hospitalization since her admission to the facility seventeen months before.

Four months later

We heard from Joy again. She had been hospitalized three times in quick succession during a one-month period. She requested to be allowed to return to the facility – for a brief stay.

In thinking about meeting her when I was invited for the admissions interview, I reflected that, yes, she cut herself or threatened to do so when she experienced extreme stress or loss of control. But she was a person with a big heart and cared for others, and she had made progress by working hard on herself during her first stay at the facility. Whatever we as a group said to her that day, I thought, I should communicate to her that I accepted her in all those aspects of her totality. It was surprising to me, then, that in the admissions interview, when I asked her what she wanted most, she replied, 'To be accepted and loved.'

Several committee members asked her questions. When she talked from her feelings of what she wanted, her feet were flat on the floor. When her feelings of defenselessness and dependence were increased in the face of harsher questions, her feet were crossed behind her, with the heels off the floor. It seemed to me that she wasn't standing or resting on her own two feet; she didn't have her feet firmly on the ground when she was in that mode of thought and being. With her feet crossed under the chair, she wasn't prepared to move. She stated that this latter posture was her favorite position for sitting. She was re-admitted by the committee.

Two months later

Joy knocked lightly on the door of my office. I knew it was she, as I had heard her speaking to someone in the hallway. I had seen her earlier in the unit and knew that she was sick and would not be going to work in the dining hall.

When she came in, I asked her about her health. Oh, she replied, she wasn't really very sick, and she wasn't suicidal. But she *was*; she needed to know where she stood in relation to suicide precaution.

When she was at our facility during her first stay, she had been on numerous suicide watches and had been told by one of the staff that she would be asked to leave the facility if she were again put on suicide watch. (The section I was assigned to has less control over its clients than the hospital at large. The clients in our section may leave the grounds and, indeed, are 'voluntary' as opposed to committed.)

Joy told me that it had helped her to be told this. And now no such ultimatum was at hand. She wasn't suicidal at the moment. But what would happen if she were?

She said she had played games in the past; she had used talk of suicidal danger as a way to get attention. To my knowledge, this was the first time she had ever admitted that. I was watching her feet. They did what they had done in the past: they were mostly curled up, crossed behind the front legs of the chair.

The days before and after her fortieth birthday were a particularly difficult time for her. To amplify her reactions, I said, 'Let's apply some pressure to slow down that aging process.' After thinking about it a little, she replied, 'It is impossible to slow down getting older.' As I tried the imaginary exercise of slowing down her forward movement in life with a 'big lever', she blurted out, 'I just want to get it over.' When her desire not to grow older was amplified, the opposite desire emerged, to get life over as quickly as possible.

I posed a question: 'Is there nothing you want to live for?' She said, no, there wasn't.

She talked of selecting a subscription from a group of about thirty magazines as part of a deal she had arranged. She said she had chosen *Writer's Digest*. She thought that would interest me. Some months ago we had talked about her doing some more writing, as she had been writing a little while living in the community. This topic now focused several real issues for her: her interest in writing, her connection with me, the therapy entailed by her writing about what had happened to her.

She talked about some of her early experiences in life. When she was three, she was beaten unmercifully by one of her uncles. This man, she has constructed since, must have told her at the same time that he was doing it 'because he loved her'. She said that she had been mixed up about what love was since that time. I pointed out that her uncle had given her a double message. He was out of control, and his statement must have been an attempt to assuage his guilt.

Throughout our talk I couldn't help but notice that her right foot never rested flat on the floor. Most of the time the toe of her shoe moved up and down. During one of the statements she was making while this movement was occurring, I stuck the toe of my shoe under the toe of her shoe and resisted the downward motion. It was quite strong. I asked her what she felt. She said, 'Up in the air. Unstable.' She said it made her feel uncertain.

I let her experience this sense of being up in the air. It was quite a strong experience for her, I knew, as her eyes became big, and she stared to one side. She became quiet and caught up in the experience. I felt the very great pressure in her foot as it strove to get to the floor. I let her stay there long enough to talk out her experience; then she became very relaxed. And the foot was flat on the floor.

She had felt 'up in the air' about her situation at the facility.

Earlier in the conversation I had tried to clarify that feeling for her by saying that if she was playing games, she would be asked to leave. If she needed our help, she would get it by whatever means were necessary, such as sick-room and suicide watch.

We talked about her suicidal thoughts. She said she was not suicidal. And the foot remained on the floor. We both noted that. I tried to show her how the body can assent to true feelings and can become an indicator if a statement stands on its merits.

When we were talking about hurting and loving, which had became bonded in her mind, I asked her if that was why she cut herself. She said that when she had last cut her arm, her 'voices' had told her that they would become silent if she cut herself. She said they hadn't done so and couldn't be trusted.

I said the voices didn't possess consciousness. They were like the body crying out. Naturally the body sought the experience of being loved, and in her mind and early experience, hurt and loving had been bonded.

Joy was playful. She enjoyed human contact. All things being normal, she would comfortably have spent her time with others, baking, sharing recipes, stories, articles. She really liked to give.

Postscript

While her primary process is to secure caring from others through hurt and the threat of hurt, her secondary process is to share, care, relate. That is the process that will get her what she really wants in life: to be loved.

In her words, 'When I stop caring for people, everything goes to the winds.' A bizarre unconscious state, impulsive and accompanied by voices, catches her up. When she finds out what she is, she can live. The dreambody gives her these signals in the lifting of her foot and even in her impulse to be scattered to the winds. The dreambody is not always tuned into life and its concerns, as we know them. But once followed, as in Joy's case, caring, creating and bonding can flow out of that experience of the body in its more dreamlike aspect.

Joy now lives in the community, in an apartment with three

other women, and has got together a little book of her own, describing her experiences. It is highly entertaining. She writes of 'my friends here at —. I can go home to visit but not too often. I want to break some of the dependency between me and my Mom. I think my future looks promising. I think in writing this book I've got a lot of feelings out to where I could look at them and now they don't seem as threatening.'

4 • Rose

At the facility we were having to watch Rose almost constantly at times. A group of us would meet her to ascertain if she was suicidal. Her depression was so extreme that she could hardly talk. When she did, she would say that she should be very accomplished. She could not even try because she needed to be the best in any field, such as music. She had always been led to believe that she had great talent.

Late winter

Rose had had a dream in which she couldn't breathe. There was another dream in which she was riding on a bus that was being driven recklessly. In a further dream she was in water: her cousin drowned; she survived. In yet another dream she went home and her parents wanted to get rid of her – they wanted her to get an apartment on her own. A trickster woman led her to a shed. She was lost. It was very difficult, and hazardous, to get back. She was afraid that she was not going to retrieve her piano from her apartment, which was occupied by someone else. She told him that he would have to give the apartment back.

Rose lay on the floor, prone. I instructed my co-therapist, a woman, to press on Rose's ribs. She placed pillows on the client's back and rested some of her weight there. My client said she had difficulty breathing. This was to amplify, to make stronger, the very first part of her dream and thereby to allow the process of the dream to dream itself on – to let the process continue itself.

Then Rose was floating high above things. Later she was in the ground with heavy rocks on top of her. (My co-therapist was still on top of her, and I had added my weight to my co-therapist's back.) Rose was dying (in her fantasy); then she was dead.

'What happens?' I asked.

'Nothing,' she answered. 'I'm dead, alone.' She continued: 'Then my spirit comes out of my body. It is up in the sky. Then my spirit slips back into the body,' she added after a pause.

I told her, 'The old person is dead.' She was infused with a new spirit. This process was like rebirth; it was related to the ritual of baptism. She would have a new garment for the new personality. I asked her to give it form artistically, and I gave her paper. She drew her enfolded body deep in the earth. A second frame showed the body near the surface. Then her soul, winged, emerged from the ground in a moment of transitory release. The body and the old ways were committed to death, a direction in which she had been aiming for some time. Jung writes:

> The imaginatio, as the alchemists understood it, is in truth the key that opens the door to the secret of the *opus* . . . it is a question of representing and realizing those greater things . . . those contents of the unconscious which are . . . not a datum of our empirical world, and therefore an a priori of archetypal character. The place or the medium of realization is neither mind or matter, but that intermediate realm of subtle reality.

He continues:

> Ruland says, 'Imagination is the star in man, the celestial or supercelestial body.' This astounding definition throws a quite special light on the fantasy processes connected with the *opus*. We have to conceive of these processes not as the immaterial phantoms we readily take fantasy-pictures to be, but as something corporeal, a 'subtle body' . . . semi-spiritual in nature. In an age when there was as yet no empirical psychology such a concretization was bound to be made, because everything unconscious, once it was activated, was projected into matter . . . The IMAGINATIO, or the act of imagining, is thus a physical activity that can be fitted into the cycle of material changes that brings these about and is brought about by them in its turn . . . Imagination is therefore a concentrated extract of the life forces, both physical and psychic.[1]

What am I to do with a fantasy like this? First of all, it is an experience. It is very different from dreaming up this or that.

The death is just like death. I hang there with her in that moment, waiting to see if she will come back.

Phenomenologically the experience is connected with all rebirth experiences. M. Esther Harding offers an ancient illustration of the person who has been reborn in baptism and who acquires a new personality, symbolized by the new garment he or she receives at the hands of an attendant. The symbolism of baptism is connected with rites of renewal in many cultures, some of whose legends speak of healing the mortally wounded. She writes:

> The font or fountain of life-giving water is known as the Uterus Ecclesia. In old churches, especially those of Norman architecture, it has the form of a hollowed-out stone. It is taught that immersion in this font endows the recipient of the sacrament with an immortal soul, just as immersion in Celtic cauldrons was thought to bring life to the dead or to bestow immortality. The idea of the mother, source of the life of the body, is here expanded into the idea of the divine mother giving birth to an immortal spirit in the mortal being, who is born a second time through immersion in the living waters of the font.[2]

Will the experience stick? Such an experience would mean something to me. But for her, a person buffeted by severe winds of mood and close to the abyss of self-doubt, will such an experience evaporate as a phantom?

Two weeks later

Rose was a little depressed; I could tell by her demeanor. She brought out drawings that showed her and a cliff. There was a plant that she could hold on to. There was a sequence: her sitting near the edge of the cliff; her being on the edge of the cliff and dangling; and her at the bottom of the cliff. In the last her body had created a small depression in the ground.

The dream she also brought seemed by its nature to be more important than the drawings. In the dream she was with her children on a barge. She swam to land with them, and she worried about whether the youngest one would manage. She swam back to the barge. And this time a woman was there with her kids. Rose's coat was missing. She looked through the woman's possessions but couldn't find it. The woman didn't seem to care. She was a contrast to Rose, a shadow figure. She didn't seem to worry much about things. She didn't need to be perfect. We talked about her a bit – how she went about things, how she felt about life, what consequences followed from her actions. At the end of the session the sparkle seemed to have returned to Rose's eyes.

Rose was a person you felt you could trust. You could picture her in a home in a normal setting, behaving like most other people. You could sense that if only circumstances were different, had been different, a normal environment would be exactly where she could be found. I would have liked to carry on our conversation. She seemed to have the capacity to be a cultivated person.

Two weeks later

Rose did not want to use her body in the work; she refused to use movement. I tended to act things out for her at her direction. We also used the mediums of dreams and drawing.

Not much had happened to her since we last met. A dream: she was inspecting a city apartment with her former husband. The ceilings were low, so low that she could barely stand up. The bedroom, she was told by the seller of the apartment, could be improved by adding skylights and raising the ceilings. If she had this work done herself, the price could be dropped by several thousands of dollars. Then she was looking for her former husband in some woods in a park. There were older habitations around.

She felt cramped. She remembered as a child feeling 'sharp and dull pains'. Where in her body were they? I asked. They were around her, she said. I had a sense that perhaps her hospitalizations and 'illness' had been caused by forces outside her.

I tried a hypothesis with her. I arranged a group of chairs

31

around her chair. I said these were her pains, sharp and dull pains in her surroundings. She seemed fearful, as if this were a representation of her situation and feelings. I had done this as a concrete representation of her words. I asked who the people in the chairs around her were, but she didn't identify any. I asked her what she wanted me to do, and she said, 'Move the chairs away. Smooth things out.' I did so, and I stood outside the path of her frontal vision. She then directed me to sit across from her.

Her husband, we had learned earlier in the sessions, had done some terrible things, after which Rose had been hospitalized. It was more than she could take. She felt very guilty about leaving the children during her illness. I tried to help her see that she probably felt she had no other way out.

We talked about the third segment of the dream, her search for her husband in the park. She said the park was the place where he threatened to commit suicide when the couple were arguing over the children and her treatment of them. I put the chairs back around her. This time she pushed them away herself.

She told me of an incident earlier in her life when she had shooed away a bear from her parents' house with a broom. She was making a connection between herself and the woman who wasn't afraid of bears.

A week later

Since the last session she had had a dream about going through her dirty laundry and separating out what was her former husband's and what was hers. Her former husband was also in the hamper. She told him to take what was his.

This seemed to follow on directly from what had happened in the last session, in which we saw that her illness and breakdown were largely the results of her husband's actions.

She was less depressed. She spoke about being very intelligent and very talented and being able to do whatever she wanted. She said she was special. It was as if she was repeating something she had been told. The words didn't seem to be supported by her own convictions.

It was clear that behind these statements lay the deep remorse that she felt for not having achieved anything or done something really special. I discussed with her the concept of living her life for the next five years; then her talent and intelligence, I said, would be able to emerge in an 'individual' way. I talked about the 'gold' inside her, indicated by such things as her spontaneous movement in the experience she had had of dying and then rising above the earth as a winged spirit. Her drawing, and the dreaming she had been doing, were part of the gold.

Tears came to her eyes when she spoke of not being able to do anything. I tried to show her that the inner gold I had mentioned *is* us; it is our essence, our most valued substance. I asked her what she was, who she was. She said she was a very intelligent and very talented person – and she would return to *person*. She said she had told the youngest of her three daughters that she was 'precious even if she couldn't do something'.

Rose was a very tall, thin woman. She looked from under her glasses as if she meant business – or could mean business if she were to be placed in a responsible position. She was certainly introverted, someone who processed through her own mind what was said to her before she responded. As time went on and she began to make contact with her creative side, she would bring in material, artwork, on which she might have worked for a whole week, and with a slight smile on her face she would communicate the story of her achievement and satisfaction.

A week later

Rose brought me a dream. In the dream she went to a female friend's house. The friend had had her child adopted because the child was blind. She had a chimpanzee in a cage.

We talked about whether it might be all right to have a child adopted by others, a matter of which Rose did not approve. I wanted her to play at being the chimp; playing roles is something she thus far had not been able to do to any great extent. I was the chimp. 'What should he do?' I asked. She said I could unlock my cage. I did so, and I came out as she directed.

What are chimps like? I had asked her earlier.

She had said, 'They are curious.'

As I played the chimp, I was curious about the room; I hopped around and looked out the window. What else should I do? I asked her.

'Chimps like to make messes,' she said. 'They might pull the books off the shelf' (about the only mess possible in that room).

This I did.

She seemed to be delighted, amazed, and to be thoroughly enjoying the chimp's actions; this was obvious from the expression of her face.

Would she like to play the chimp?

No.

Would she like to pull down the books?

Yes. 'And throw them around the room?' she asked. She had not been able to make messes in her mother's home.

I asked my co-therapist if she would like to make a mess. She said she would like to but she declined.

I have not told you much about Rose's outer life. She worked in one of the workshops of the facility, an art print shop. Normally the clients worked several hours a day in the morning during the five-day working week. Rose had been putting in extra hours, working regularly about seven hours a day. She was also making plans to apply for a work-training program when she left the facility. She hoped to gain effective training for future work. She showed us her matting work. It was exceptional.

At that time Rose had an important court date coming up that involved the future of her youngest daughter, who was currently under the protective custody of the state in a juvenile treatment facility. Rose had strong mixed feelings about her daughter; she wanted her daughter at home with her again, but her daughter was often in trouble, and then it was almost too much for Rose to cope with.

Two weeks later

Rose's dreams had been as follows.

First dream: 'I am pregnant.'

Second dream: 'I make love with a guy whom I met when I was in the hospital; he had been an alcoholic.'

Third dream: 'My piano teacher gossips about someone.'

It turned out that the piano teacher was an impeccable person, someone almost perfect in Rose's eyes. This helped to create a scene in which the piano teacher was acted out: she was trying to maintain the perfectionistic quality of Rose's projection, while at the same time revealing her all too human weaknesses for such things as gossip. The tension of this made Rose aware of the other side of her idol, which she had to acknowledge.

A week later

Rose spoke about working seven hours a day in the workshop. She also brought a series of art prints she had made for a college class. Her demeanor was energetic.

In the first dream that she discussed she was nursing a baby; the baby was not hers. She felt she must hide (her feeling was that others might think she was weird). She also told us that she enjoyed nursing her own babies. She liked feeling close.

What did it mean that the baby was not hers? She picked this point up when I mentioned that in her former dream she had been pregnant. I wanted her to see the dream not literally but symbolically. I talked with her about the child as a symbol of potential development, as a symbol of the Self. The Self is that total quality that includes limitations, faults, the murky quality of motivation. The Self represents the wholeness that we had talked about in previous sessions, which is in contrast to perfectionism as a goal of personality. She admitted, late in the session, that she had wanted to hide this dream even from me. Her mother would regard it as weird that she was paying attention to

Self, nurturing her inner life, discussing her dreams with me, taking account of her feelings. Her taking care of herself was not for public view. She seemed to assent to such perspectives and understandings.

In the second dream she rode a horse. Then she tried on baby shoes for a boy. They were too wide for her. She could make the association between horse and instinct and said she had a healthy relationship with one person with whom she hoped to live. Her feet were narrow. She associated trying on the shoes with trying to be a regular person. A regular person, she said, would not go to the hospital but would deal with suffering alone. In the dream she was trying to fit into baby shoes.

In the last dream she brought she wanted to run to her former psychiatrist; then she discovered a blind man and peeled potatoes for him. The psychiatrist reminded her of her boyfriend, the man whom she hoped to live with. She felt about the second part of the dream that if she did something practical, it would help her get out of her depression. She also drew a lesson from the dream: that things are not as difficult for her as they are for some people – for instance, those who lack physical sight.

I asked her if she would like me to play the blind man. She said yes. She told me, 'I am in a box and surrounded by darkness, but I have my other senses. As for the blind man, I find myself accepting that he has problems too.' I asked her who else was in the room. She mentioned the co-therapist: 'She is a nice person.' I asked Rose if she felt close to her. 'No. There is very little exchange on the unit,' she told me.

I indicated to her some of the nice things which happened to me as a blind man. 'People come up, and they want to take my hand and be warmer towards me than they feel they can be in ordinary life. There is a closeness to walking across the street with such a person.'

The play came to an end.

I asked her if she wanted to touch the blind man's hand. She said she did. She then spoke of a former therapist who would squeeze her shoulder when she left his room; she said she didn't remember anything he said, but she always remembered that squeeze. And a woman therapist had hugged her. Rose wanted to be close to people. She acknowledged this and said the baby in her first dream didn't resist.

As the session came to a close I took her hand to shake it. The grip was very strong. My co-therapist also hugged Rose, saying she had wanted to do that for a long time.

One week later

She came in and immediately pulled out a little piece of paper from the back pocket of her jeans: her dreams.

'I have braces on my teeth, but I don't need them. The braces make the teeth straight – but they are already straight,' she explains. Teeth enable her to eat, which gives her pleasure and sustains her body. When I echoed her words and linked them with her understanding of her teeth she said, 'I don't need to be here any more.' A third element of the dream was that one tooth was loose. She feared at times that all her teeth would fall out. Another element was that she said one tooth hurt, but the dentist said there was nothing wrong with it.

She spoke of a dream in which she was being ignored by her best friend from high school. However, in the dream her best friend's mother was concerned for her feelings and put her arm around her and said she could stay with her. I played Rose. I said my co-therapist was her girl friend's mother. I went over and sat down beside my co-therapist, and we pretended she had put her arm around me. We talked. I said how much it hurt that my best friend ignored me. The mother said she cared for me. I said I was really upset. She said, 'You can come and live with me' (as in the dream).

Rose burst out, '*My* mother wouldn't let me.'

I echoed this to my co-therapist, who said, 'You are an adult. If you want to come live with me, well, then you can!'

I told Rose that the dream had given her the good mother. She had shouted from the sidelines that she liked me (really herself). I said that with a good mother inside her now she could do things, and they wouldn't go wrong. (By 'good mother' I meant an image of mother as a psychological personage who does not reject and offers sympathy and a protective place to stay.)

Two weeks later

My co-therapist had told me before the session that Rose had not been balanced the evening before.

Her dream was as follows.

She was on a bus with her friend. She had gone to the dentist. He told her there was a problem with the roots of her teeth. He said that her teeth would fall out and she would have to have dentures. In the next segment of the dream she had a miscarriage. She was in a car with her former husband. He was driving. She was in the back seat, where some bean plants were growing from the floor: she would eventually can the beans.

The dream about the teeth pertained to her fear of losing (conscious) control. Teeth had been discussed before. She was feeling pressured into accepting self-medication, and she was not sure she would not use it to harm herself through an overdose, as she had done before. The dream showed however, that she would get dentures, teeth which would not become loose and fall out.

The dream miscarriage could be associated with her former husband as well as with harm to her children and her mental health. He was asking her for a divorce and had requested more of their possessions, so that, if she went along with his request, she might be reduced to 'free food' and canning foods herself – her association with the dream image. I supported her in getting what she needed from the divorce in order to support herself.

A week later

Rose was on suicide watch. The loosening of her teeth had become a reality. She had talked about plans to store away medications and take them all at once. And she had attempted to run off.

Her dream. She was in the water surrounded by headhunters.

They were going to kill her. There was nothing she could do. She reported other dreams, one a week before, with a similar theme.

She showed signs of agitated depression. Her former husband wanted her to take over responsibility for her elder daughter, who is a management problem and a juvenile delinquent. Rose felt guilty about not being able to handle her daughter at that time, and her guilt had been increased by a staff member who had urged her to assume her responsibilities.

There seemed to be no choice but to go into the dream. I asked her if she wanted to, and she agreed. I asked her where to put chairs (natives) around her. She directed me. She said my co-therapist was one of the natives.

I asked her to direct parts of what followed. I said I would play her, and she could be the headhunter. I tried everything I could think of to appeal to my would-be 'assassin'. In the guise of the headhunter her voice asserted itself with crisp matter-of-factness, which completely demolished any appeal I attempted. Finally, without much delay, she shot the poison arrow. There was no antidote, according to her. My body was thrown into the river and would have reached the ocean, but a piranha ate it. My head was placed on a pole and shrunk.

I asserted that the spirit was still over my head. I asked her to take the spirit where she wanted it to go, and I gave her my tie. She led me to another part of the big room. 'Where am I?' I asked. She couldn't tell me.

Then she said I was in a meadow. The sun was shining. There were trees. She said I was a butterfly. For a long time I waved and flew around. She said she felt sleepy. I said it was OK if she went to sleep. She didn't quite manage to fall asleep at this point. I said the butterfly was the symbol of rebirth and the soul. I 'landed' near her. This time she went to sleep for a little while. I folded my wings and waited. When she talked again, she *directed* that the butterfly be in a body. I stood before her. Her soul and body had come together again.

She was silent. I said there was something I felt like doing: putting a gift on the altar. She said she would like to dedicate herself. She would like to 'help other people'.

I put the chairs back. Then I clapped my hands once in front of her face. I sat in a chair along the wall parallel to hers. What was I thinking? she asked. I said that I was feeling that I too must make an offering and that she should draw or describe what had taken place. She should remember what happened between her and people. We would meet again the next day.

A week later

In this session Rose said that she was now able to say that she hadn't been happy the week before that I had kept her alive (i.e., on suicide watch at the institution). She was happy and sparkling. (I think she bounced back quickly from being really low because her psyche had been touched.)

She brought a dream. In the dream she had a creature in her hands. It was slippery. It was difficult to hold on to. However, if she fed it, it would get bigger and easier to hold.

She associated the slippery creature with the way she had got out of the difficult situation of the previous week. She was having trouble holding on to that. But if she fed it, nurtured it, then it could get bigger and not be so difficult to hold.

The creature was a baby creature. It was a frog. Frogs evolve from eggs to tadpoles to frogs. There is in their process a metamorphosis like that of the butterfly of the previous week's experience for Rose. Her word for this was 'change'.

The setting of this dream was a department store, where there was an escalator. She associated this with her mood swings. I had the feeling that if she could stay with the process, nurture this new way of handling her depression, then she would be less subject to terrible mood swings.

I talked to her about relating to change, flowing with it and accepting it. We looked at some of the changes of her life.

The way for her to nurture the new creature was, in her words, to work with me. She could continue to draw the process. The drawing she brought with her that time was very powerful.

That session meant a great deal to me. There was a striking 'inner' quality to her picture. Also she seemed to be grateful to be alive. She recognized that there were times when her judgment was not to be trusted, when she was extremely depressed. She was responsive to the dream work. I believe she sensed that there was in this work of following her process something genuine to offset her vulnerability to mood disorder.

A further note. Before the session started she entered my office and saw all my papers scattered about in piles. I told her I was going to make a presentation the next day about the process. She said, 'Oh, you can talk about me.' I sensed giving on her part. It helped me a great deal. Her attitude, and the synchronicity of it, inspired me.

Some three weeks later

We came to the last session. She was to leave next week. She was to start a new job with a friend and to have her oldest daughter at home for a while on a trial basis. There would be many changes. Her dream of the night before was of a duck and a drake and six little ducks. Then she crossed some water and was playing a piano. First she made mistakes, then her playing improved.

She saw the ducks living on the water and on land and flying in the air as change. It was change which she had derived as the essence of her former dreams and images of the butterfly and frog. These images of change were what the unconscious was giving her to face events to come, images for her nature and for the cycles of life, which for her were more pronounced than others. I reminded her of her recent experience of being completely subdued, and of the experience of death, which was then followed by rebirth. By following her process, rather than taking her period of depression literally or statically, she could find the rebirth which followed.

I gave her a beautiful photograph of a butterfly from China. She thanked me; I thanked her for letting me share her process of the butterfly.

Pan, nature itself, and play were needed to understand and participate in Rose's process. Over and over again she dreamed of me in this role. I played her dreams for her because of her reluctance to act them out herself. I was the friendly chimp, ecstatically hopping around, getting into mischief, making a mess and being curious. Play was the secondary process in many instances. It held the key for the girl who was immobilized by her own expectations of her talents and specialness.

At desperate times, such as in the dream about the headhunter, I jumped into the water with her, so to speak. I had no other choice. It was a great experience for me, a last-resort effort, as I didn't know where it would end.

Nature, natural processes, the liveliness of animals and insects, were the unconscious's mighty answer to her withdrawal, depression and desire to give up. Frog spawn that will become a swimming water creature and later a hopping frog, a butterfly metamorphosing from the cocoon to the imago to the beautiful creature of the sky, Rose's drawings and the liveliness and spirit inherent there – the animal images of process were mirror images of the attention she paid to psyche in dreams, to working on dreams and drawing them.

Process is a fluid way of describing a pattern. The pattern in much of Rose's work was of death and rebirth. Can we call that a life process? Indeed. Only with death, or the radical change of the old, is the way made possible for the new. She was stuck in death, in hospitalization over a period of many years. When the pattern of death could be lived at the point of active imagination, when she couldn't breathe and that pattern was allowed to unfold, then she discovered spirit. It was capable both of being free of the body and re-entering it to infuse it with life.

As I think back on these moments of drama I remember feeling in awe. When someone who has been so depressed responds to such imagery, then I can only wonder at the self-regulating powers of the psyche/body. Such were my feelings, and such has been my impetus to write this book. These things really do exist. They are not dusty ideas; there are basic processes at work in life. When, through dreambody work, they are released to complete themselves, then we have a new being; maybe a slippery creature at first but one that can grow into the stuff of the subtle body, the immortal substance of the alchemists.

Rose wrote a year later, in essence: 'I am fine, and I am not fine.' She continued: 'What I do isn't that important. Or how smart or talented I am. It's my very being – my essence – that's important. I am then truly free – and then more able to love and care for others. It's not what other people do or how smart they are that makes them special to me – it's their essence.'

I would like to offer some more explicit observations about channel and dreambody theory for the clinician and interested layperson. At the beginning point of our work, and during her second suicidal crisis at the facility, Rose was in an extreme state. From the beginning of that first session one might have concluded that she had nothing to live for. Death was very strong in the dream about the headhunter; indeed, when she later played this role, her manner was unrelenting. In the guise of death, she was immovable.

Death is not the end in dreambody theory. From dreams there are clear indications that we have connections with life, or lives, prior to our own and that when life as we know it ends other processes may go on. One of Mindell's insights is that the multi-channeled perceptual system of the dreambody may be eternal, while the body itself is not.

Joy and Rose had out-of-body experiences of being in the air, a clear indication of what we are calling the dreambody. Such experiences are connected with life, both before and after our own. Dreambody is the spirit.

Dreambody is also the illness. The dreambody announces itself through illness, saying through it, 'The way you are living is out of line.'

In extreme states death comes along as a kind of final punctuation. The image of death is present in every illness, ready to take over when the dreambody cannot fuse with the physical body: death is near when we do not follow our process. Switching channels is the cue to follow the process again.

Rose's dreambody was making itself felt in her inability to breathe. We amplified the experience by leaning on her. This proprioceptive experience switched her out of the verbal–

auditory channel, where for her there was no hope, only unrealized, unrealistic expectations. In turn, once she felt that pressure on her chest proprioception switched to her visual channel. It was a vision of her dreambody, her eternal self, that showed her real nature to be like a spirit, a dreambody. All her subsequent internal images of butterflies and frogs speak of this quality, something that is in the body but assumes different forms, so that the body can never finally be identified with it.

The psychotic state is the one in which new and startling awareness is possible. There dreambody, in the company of death (another of the images of Mercurius), offers its awareness. In Rose's case the freed spirit moved spontaneously into the real body, infusing it again with life, with spirit. That was her process. As Arnold Mindell has written, 'A disease may be its own healing process.'

Process-oriented psychology follows dreams in the body; follows channel switches and amplifies them; watches altered states of consciousness reorganize life. If people are trained to work with borderline and psychotic states, such as major depression, through process-oriented psychology, we are going to develop very different perspectives on the treatment of persons with these disorders.

A final note. When Rose (acting as death) wouldn't let me (acting as Rose) live, she dreamed me as her spirit. I hung over the decapitated head impaled on the pole. When asked what she wanted to do with the spirit, she got up and led it around, arriving at a meadow. There was a switch from verbal–auditory to kinesthetic, a channel that had been woefully inactive up to that point. Once there, the dreambody or process took over, organizing the new life symbolized in the butterfly and its actions.

5 • Monie

Monie could have been a model. She had dark hair and dark eyes. Her face was strong and had character to it. It didn't seem appropriate that she was a mental patient.

Monie's mother and brother were visiting her at the facility. Some members of staff were present at the end of a meeting. Monie shouted at her mother angrily, 'I can never have a baby,' and she went to the door of the conference room and said that her mother had told her that she was defective, had implied that she wouldn't get well. I called her back into the group.

Soon most of my colleagues excused themselves and left the room so that I could work with Monie, her mother and her brother. I requested that a counselor stay behind. Monie turned her back to the rest of the circle and sat with her side towards me. I turned and faced as she was facing. I also called attention to the fact that she had her back towards her mother. She picked up the body signal.

It wasn't long before Monie was asking me to play her part. She directed a role play. She began telling me what I felt – that is, directing her own thoughts at me. I repeated her statements, not exactly, but reflecting them so that she could hear them.

Monie said: 'My mother and father are separated. My mother committed me to mental health.' She was tapping her heel. I asked her to tap her heel harder and to tell me what it felt like. She looked surprised at first, but she went along with the exercise, and she said it felt exciting. She recalled a trip to Barbados with her father.

Monie had often left the room to get water, especially at the beginning of the session, and she had always returned. At this point she went to the door and said, 'We are now in reality.' I asked her to rejoin us in the circle and tell each of us what it was like now that we were in reality. She looked at me and said, 'You will stop dreaming.' I asked her what she had to say to her brother, and she asked, 'Are you OK, Rick?' Then she looked at the counselor and said, 'You're responsible for your own reality.' When she looked at her mother, she said again, 'You are responsible for your own reality.' Each of these statements indicated that she was to some extent aware that she was responsible for her reality, that she did too much daydreaming and that she was really concerned about her brother. She was in reality.

At this point she looked at the book her mother had brought, *Schizophrenia*, and she asked her mother about the book. It was an indirect way of asking for the book. Her mother said that the book had to go home that day but that she might look for a copy to send Monie. Monie got a little angry again and said that she didn't want her mother to send her anything else.

At this point she seemed to be thinking. After a few moments I asked what she was thinking. She said that she would like to buy her mother a bouquet of flowers. I suggested that she could go outside and pick some flowers, as there were no florists near by. She took to this idea and left the room. She came back in about five minutes and said she couldn't find any flowers. I went to the window and pointed out a spot where I could see some from the window. I told her that when she returned her mother would be there waiting for her but the counselor and I would have gone.

I asked Monie's mother to do exactly what she felt like doing when her daughter returned with the flowers, hoping that the mother might take this as a signal to hug her child. Her mother told me later that Monie had brought some flowers for her and that she had pressed them in the book and was taking them back home to California with her.

A few months later

Monie came into my office. She was upset. She said she felt very tense. I asked her if anything in particular had happened. She said that in her workshop three of the other clients worked in one section and she in another. She said they never made any overtures to her; she, by contrast, was always making approaches to them. She asked me why that was so. I said that many of the clients at the facility are withdrawn. That seemed to make sense to her. Then she asked, 'Am I withdrawn?' I said that sometimes she was. She talked about periods of changing energy. She spoke about being slow in the morning and so active in the evening that she felt a little crazy.

She then proffered the information that as a young person she had not had such fluctuations of energy. She described a summer-camp experience in which she had felt negatively about people but had not spoken about her feelings. She said, 'After that, I got catapulted into it' (referring to her mental disorder). She asked, 'Do you think it is possible that it all started that way?'

I said, 'Yes.'

She was overjoyed, suddenly so energetic that she rushed from the room. It was as if all the negativity towards people into which she had been catapulted *was* the mental illness.

The meeting in which we involved Monie's family continued to be a springboard of rapport. We often saw each other in the hall and spoke sporadically. Those meetings, while brief, often had a central content of some significance. I had the feeling that I was playing the role of therapist almost *in absentia*. A process had started, and it continued without regular sessions.

Monie took great strides when she walked. She moved quickly. Her conversation was like that too. She would ask a pithy question, and when one had got out a few words she would be on her way again, saying as she left that the reply made sense and implying that it had satisfied her.

About seven months after the first session

She was upset and confused. She talked about her awareness of her sexuality when she was a Girl Scout and about hiding it self-consciously because her mother was present. When she was in high school her sexuality developed, and she sought men in the streets; her mother had her committed to a mental hospital.

Monie used to sling her arms down beside her when she sat in a chair. We went into that gesture. Ah, it was her mother who threw her hands down by her side and behind her. The voice of her mother: 'You can't do things like they could be done. You must do them like they should be.' Monie said, 'My mother is perfect,' in a tone of despair and frustration, as if she were saying, 'Where does that leave me?' But her mother wasn't perfect.

It was through this process that I became aware of some aspects of Monie's sexuality. I couldn't get her to move out of her chair. I went over to the door. I opened it and said, 'We are going to let this little girl walk through her life.' When I played at holding the hand of the imaginary child beside me (ten or eleven years old), Monie exclaimed in great surprise, 'She is happy!' She saw herself there. She had forgotten that there was a time of life during which she was happy.

Two weeks later

Monie was sitting in my room when my co-therapist and I arrived. Her eyes were made up, and her glasses were pushed back on her hair over her forehead. We both commented that she looked beautiful, following up an image of herself that had come up the week before.

She asked at the beginning of the session, 'Where does my self-hatred come from?' She offered the suggestion that it came from hurt, fear and unacceptable realities.

I seized one of the chairs that were around the edge of the large room and placed it in the middle. I turned it over quite roughly, and I said, 'This is hurt.' I was going to go for 'fear' and 'unacceptable realities' in the same way, but Monie got up and pulled another chair into the center of the room, behind the first one. She said this was love. It pointed diagonally away from where I was sitting. She sat down in the chair and talked from there. I sensed that it was a relief for her not to look at me directly and not to be seen. She asked if there was such a thing as love; she talked about the trust in people that she was feeling.

48

Then she took her original place on the small couch by the door. She said, 'You guys are really sincere, aren't you?' She added, 'This therapy is good.'

She then talked about the load on her shoulders. I asked my co-therapist to be the load. My co-therapist complied, without my specifically directing her what to do, and she leaned her forearms on Monie's back. 'What is back there?' I asked Monie.

She said, 'Two women whose bodies are together, and a picture of two persons copulating which belonged to a cousin.' The first image provoked the response 'Yucko' and the second prompted a question: 'Why are men like that?'

I said I would act these images out, as I had done with the chairs. I was too vague about what I would do: she was threatened by the material and left, half-way through the hour. She said she might or might not return.

When Monie came back a few minutes later I remarked that she had changed her clothes: she had replaced a tight, flowery blouse with a loose khaki-colored man's shirt. She said she didn't feel safe. I assured her that she was safe with us.

I tried to explain that sometimes women turned to other women for caring, love and even physical contact. I said men did the same. She asked, almost in panic, 'Are you saying I am a lesbian?' I tried to help her see the most symbolic element of her image, caring between women.

She had asked me at the very first of our meetings, 'What is an archetype?' She had seen the word on the cover of the journal *Spring*, which was lying on the couch. I now tried to return to this and to refer to an incident that had occurred in an early session.

At that time she had seen my co-therapist, sitting beside her, as going up in flames. The fantasy threatened her. This came up because I had asked her at the beginning of the session if she was feeling anything in her body and if she had had any dreams. Her answer was no, but she said she had been fantasizing. I asked her to tell me about the fantasies, and that was when her acknowledgment of self-hatred, hurt, fear and unacceptable realities emerged. I went over to my colleague and said that she was my friend and nothing would happen to her, but we would let the flames consume her and see what happened.

The remains of the body were lying there. What would Monie like to do with them? 'There is the ocean,' she said. But she took the remains and put them in an ashtray on the table. I then acted the scene for her. I took the ashes of my colleague to the ocean. I performed a ritual, saying I was reuniting the remains of my friend with the ocean and the cosmos. Monie moved around in her chair and clasped her hands together; a smile spread across her face.

So I had occasion, all these months later, to return to the topic of archetypes and the use of ritual to deal with powerful and threatening fantasy when it came to the sexual images she was carrying on her back. She wanted to rush from the room, as she usually did when confronted with difficulty. I said we weren't through. The chairs were still in the middle of the room. Were we going to leave them there? 'Yes,' she said. Then she turned the chair of hurt right side up and moved 'love' into the ring. She muttered that she probably didn't do this as well as professionals.

A week later

Monie stated that she did not know if she could stand the pain of being alive. I had come to this crossroads before with people in extreme emotional states. I wondered then, as I had before, whether Monie would be able to go on with the work as it led towards what Michlem, a psychiatrist and Jungian analyst, calls the 'intolerable image'.[1]

Three weeks later

Eight years before Monie had been told by a psychiatrist, wrongly, that she was schizophrenic and would never get better. I and my co-therapist regarded her condition as related to her use of mescaline when she was about eighteen. She had spent her time in institutions since then and had an extremely low self-concept.

She told me, after I offered to play her, that I was mentally retarded, a cripple and an animal. I acted out these roles successively. It was afterwards, when I had sat down, that she said, 'I am afraid of myself.' I proceeded to play that out as well. I took a chair and put it in front of where she was sitting and said, 'Now *I* am your Self. You are Monie.' (The Self is something different from Monie; she is afraid of it.) I said, 'Monie, look at the Self you are afraid of.'

I sat in the chair in front of her and echoed her words. It emerged that 'herself', her Self, was 'beauty'.

As she talked, she said she had once felt beautiful. My co-therapist and I told her she was beautiful. She tried to reject this self-concept, but she was listening. It seemed to be one of the places to work: the secondary process was to be beautiful.

Ten days later

She saw me in the snack shop. She said, 'David, you really helped me.'

I knew the last session had been important for her. I had wondered at the time, and afterwards, if facing her fantasies would relieve her from an inner pressure that seemed to drive her to leave meetings. Facing the threatening could help her work on the fear that leads to self-hatred.

Three days later

Monie was picking at her skin around one of the nails of her right hand. We went into that. It was a scab, and she was trying to clean it up. All the people at the treatment facility were scabs, and people on the outside were loving and lovable. What is a scab? A healing thing. What do people who are ailing and healing deserve? Respect and time to get better.

She was a healing thing. She deserved time to get better. She reported that she was trying to like herself and to love herself.

'Let's try to get inside that scab,' I told Monie.

'Ugh,' she responded.

'Well, let's go in with a microscope. What's happening down there?'

'There is an army of cells.'

'What kind of cells are they?'

'There are white and red ones.'

'What do the white ones do?'

'They fight infection.'

'What do the red ones do?'

'They bring oxygen and hemoglobin. They make the injured skin start to look beautiful again.'

'Really?'

'All that happens if you let the natural process take place and don't pick at the healing thing, the scab.'

She paused and relaxed for a while.

We went on to talk about the good people and the bad people who had featured in Monie's initial mention of the scab. She asked for more of this. I told her that the good and the bad was in all of us, those in the community and those in the hospital. I repeated something she had told me the day before – that she had a body, was a body. I said that was wonderful. She corrected me: it wasn't *wonderful*; it just *was*. I suggested to her that many of the ordinary people she imagined out there in the community had probably never had the experience that she had described.

Monie stayed for the best part of an hour. The session had run its natural course.

Five weeks later

Monie talked about a home visit to Centralia that coming weekend. (Centralia is in another part of the state, near a large city.) She said she planned to see a person with whom she used to design fashion clothes. She hoped they would still have a relationship and that he and she could design the kind of clothing she likes because no one else was interested in just that form of dress. If her plan failed, she said, she might commit suicide.

We talked about what her real goals were behind this: to be a designer, to live a normal life. I could tell that this objectification didn't touch her. I suggested that she could follow this alternative scheme rather than resting everything on the weekend ahead, that she was setting the stakes pretty high.

I went over to the shelves and got some books. I said, 'Put these on the floor in a big stack. These are the stakes.' She heard 'mistakes'. I said, 'All right, let's look at these mistakes.' I picked up one of the books and asked which one it was. Monie said it was the time she had threatened her mother, many years before. I asked her if she could let it go. She did. The second book she saw as a mistake that her father had made, which had resulted in his being asked to leave their home. 'Could you forgive your father that mistake?' I asked.

'What does it mean "to forgive"?' The dictionary showed no complicated meaning. 'Yes, I can forgive him,' she said.

'If you can forgive him, that means that we can take five books and put them back on the shelves because if you show forgiveness to him, then you can forgive yourself.'

With the next book Monie forgave her mother for being too good. She dealt rather quickly with mistakes made with or by men. I could see, as I took the books up and she disposed of them one way or another, that these experiences were real to her.

Monie had said earlier in the session that she would like to leave the facility and to move back to Centralia. She worked for the full hour. Before she left she promised me that she would not harm herself that weekend.

Later she dropped into my office and said she didn't want to live with sick people much longer.

A week later

Monie burst into tears. It seemed she had smoked pot during the weekend of her home visit, which had not gone well. She had been over-stimulated by the big city, and there had been a scene with her sister.

She was very upset. In her eyes her brother and sister were great successes, whereas she felt she had wasted the last eighteen years of her life. She said, 'I hate being me.' I tried to play her and asked her to tell me what she hated. She appeared to have doubts about my method.

At one point she made some reference to 'warrior', maybe to having been a warrior. I asked her to show me.

She said, 'This is ridiculous.'

I told her I could try to show her a warrior's stance, which I did. Then she tried her own way. She spun away from me and moved across the room. I was surprised by the power of her steps and her gracefulness. She was surprised too and said, 'This is fun.' Thereafter her body pose was quite different, and she moved around the room in a relaxed way, as if her personality showed through her body. As we discussed my reactions to her movement, she would trail into negativity, but I kept talking about what had come up – power, will (she had identified this with another gesture) and love. At those moments her concentration had been focused on herself rather than on others.

A week later

Monie talked about being an ordinary person, and she explored questions of a kind that related to ordinary events. The questions were simple and innocent and her style and manner of talking those of a young girl finding out the most basic things of life. She directed her questions to my co-therapist, a woman. I asked Monie if she would like a session with my colleague on her own. She took up the idea enthusiastically.

Two weeks later

Monie reported a dream in which her family had gathered together. Each person was behaving normally and naturally, including her. Everyone was all right. Monie had always considered herself a failure and her perception of herself had been debilitating. The dream portrayed a new possibility.

She reported this feeling in workshop. She said, 'It is great to be alive, overwhelmingly good to be alive.' She was developing a very positive transference to my co-therapist.

The next day

She came to my office to inquire about a comment I had made about feeling alpha waves when I woke from an afternoon nap. In passing I mentioned that happiness is the natural state of the mind.[2] She said, 'Oh, it is fear which drives it away and lets depression in.'

Four weeks later

Monie remarked, 'I am coming out of my shell.' She said she was learning to 'simply live'. I asked her what this meant, and she said, 'To take one feeling at a time.' She mentioned her fear that the world would blow itself up. I connected the two ideas and said that as more people tried to learn to live simply, this would be a deterrent to nuclear war.

When Monie was talking about her recent feelings I asked her if she could locate them in her body. She pressed on her chest bone and the upper part of her stomach, just below her rib cage. I asked her to tell me what was in there. She said, 'I really want a boyfriend.' Her arms stuck out at the elbows and moved upwards in an arc. I explained what she had said and what I had seen. I asked my co-therapist to go around on the other side of her. I went to her right side.

I instructed her to raise her arms again at the same point as before while I repeated her statements. My co-therapist and I applied slight pressure, resistance, at the upper arc of her motion. She came out with: 'I could be lucky.'

I sat down opposite her. I repeated the whole process. She broke out laughing when I stated, 'I could be lucky.' But her expression altered. She said, 'This could all change very suddenly.' I repeated the whole sequence of words, and this time indicated that a black cloud had come over her with the thought that this moment of happiness might not last for ever. She thought that was enormously funny. I connected the awareness of this moment, and the process, with her tendency to be up and down in very quick succession.

Monie said, 'My dad is here.'

I said, 'Well, let's invite him in.' Again there was uproarious laughter on her part. She set up her own role play and held a conversation with him that lasted perhaps five minutes. She took his part as well. Then I decided to move into the empty chair in order actively to play his part. She had first represented some judgment about her not talking. Things had then begun to flow. Now she began to compare herself with her siblings, as she had done many times before. 'What would you like him to say?' I asked her.

She said, 'That I'm OK for just living.'

'You're OK for just living.'

She dashed from the room.

Five weeks later

Monie said she wasn't in reality today. She said she didn't want to stay for the session; she wanted to die. She asked, 'What use is this treatment anyway?' Even her father was negative about her. She left the room, went to the water fountain and returned.

She said, 'Tell me what my problem is, why I am here.'

I took one of the chairs from the circle and put it in the middle of the room. I said, 'This is you as an adolescent. You kick up things a bit. Your mother has to come and get you in the middle of the night.' (She had done a bit more than most adolescents, but many adolescents have a stormy period in which they fight with their parents and families.) I took another chair, identical in appearance, and put it beside the first one. I said, 'This is another girl, eighteen years old. She, like a lot of adolescents, has sown wild oats and fought with her family. But there is a difference.'

Then I told her a story. I have now forgotten exactly where I first heard it, but it is from Tibet.

Two monks were walking along, and they came to a river. There was a woman in some distress, and she needed to get over to the other side. It was strictly forbidden for a monk at that time even to look at a woman, but the first monk said to her, 'Climb on,' and he carried her on his shoulders as he waded across the ford. The two monks said farewell and went on their own way.

After several hours, the second monk broke the silence and said, 'You carried that woman across the river.'

The first monk replied, 'And you, my brother, have been carrying her ever since.'

I explained to her that the difference between her and the girl who had had a wild adolescence was that she, at thirty-six, was still holding on to the experience, still carrying it. The other girl had gone on to different things. What's more, she, Monie, wasn't crazy, and she wasn't schizophrenic.

At this point she got up and paced around the room. I had been pacing and talking quite loudly. Now she was getting angry. I stayed with her anger and didn't try to moderate it. Then she said again, 'I feel like just dying,' and she left the room. This time she was gone a long time. I told my colleague that it was better for her to be angry in our therapy room than on the unit.

When she returned she said, 'Nobody cares for me.'

I said I did.

She asked, 'Do you think I could say something to you I don't say to anyone?'

'You could,' I said.

She asked, 'What does it mean to be subservient?'

I explained. She asked if this was a good state for women. My co-therapist and I said no. She said, 'I am not subservient to me.' I played at being angry with her and repeated her statement with force. She added, 'I am not sweet.' I affirmed this. She was taken aback.

I said, 'I accept you as one who is not sweet and who is not subservient.'

She asked, 'Where do you see me going?' I tried to play a game with her and put my eye to an imaginary telescope, asking what lay in the future. She was irritated by this, so we talked instead. I said I didn't see her staying much longer at our institution, where, as she had just reported, men treated her in such a way that she had started to believe that subservience was one of her characteristics. I said I could see her washing dishes and living in a school for kids.

She got very excited. 'Do you actually know about such a place?' she asked. I said I did, but I hesitated to raise her hopes because there was only a 15 per cent chance that the plan could succeed. I said I had even dreamed about it.

When I saw her in the hallway just after the session she thanked me for the meeting.

A week later

She had come to my office earlier, saying she would like to find out if she really could leave. I said we could talk about that later. At the beginning of the session I decided instead to ask her what she wanted to work on. She said, 'I don't trust myself. It even hurts in my body.'

I asked, 'Where in your body?'

She said, 'In the parts which are most vulnerable to me.'

I asked, 'Is that in your feminine parts?'

And she said, 'Yes.'

'Your feminine parts hurt.'

'Yes. The babysitter told us to take off our clothes and get on top of him in the bed. I wouldn't. My parents came in. They smoothed over the whole thing.'

'Are you sure you didn't do anything?'

'I don't want to think about it.'

'Children can't be blamed for this sort of thing.'

'Really? Why not?'

'Children do things people who are older than them tell them to do, even if they feel they are wrong.'

'Oh.'

'How old were you?'

'I was four.'

'What happened?'

'I really don't want to think about it.'

'It could help to go into it. I've seen other people your age and older who've had these things happen to them when they were children. And it did help them to talk about them. It's maybe where it all started.'

'I was on the beach at Corpus Christi. I was singing a song. I was happy. I wrote to my brother about it later.'

'What happened?'

'I need to get a drink of water. I'll be back.'

'I'll be you. And [pointing to my colleague] you be the babysitter. Is that OK with you, Monie?'

'Now I'm four years old, and I'm singing and happy.'

I strolled along. Then I lay down on the floor.

She said, 'The beach is behind me. The sky is blue, and there are flowers.'

I stretched out my arm and bent my knees in a completely relaxed way.

She said, 'That's it. I see it now . . . Oh, yucko. Oh, yucko.' As her re-enactment of the experience continued, she said, 'I hate you! I hate you!' Her voice, directed at the babysitter, became quite agitated and strong. She asked, 'Can I leave now?'

I said, 'I'd like you to stay. Perhaps we can just be quiet for a bit.' I decided to sit on the floor in a meditative pose.

Monie was pacing back and forth by the window. She asked me if this bothered me. I said no.

I said, 'You have been suffering because of this experience all this time and because of your mother's marriage' (which she had described as twenty-three years of unhappiness).

'They told me once in Arkansas that I should suffer,' she said. 'It would enable me to get to happiness.'

'Suffering is not the way to happiness,' I countered. 'Happiness is the natural state of the mind.'

She had said earlier that as a child she had stood under an apple tree and told her father, 'I will never be happy.'

A single memory such as this one from Monie's childhood can send someone with a formerly active psychosis into a terrible and terrifying world again. Why did it not happen in this case? If we go back and look at the process, we may find some clues.

I knew that Monie had absolute trust in the work we were doing together and in me. Where the process holds sway, I, the therapist, have an unshakeable trust in what unfolds. The process was then at the point of the unthinkable thought, the intolerable image. The action was meant to go on. She was on the edge of awareness – an awful edge.

I let myself be her for a minute and acted out the state of mind implied by her memory of herself as a four-year-old. Then another memory came up from the bottom of the sea: 'Oh, yucko. Oh, yucko.' (Monie had first used this childish expression six months earlier, when my co-therapist had leaned on her back.) 'I hate you! I hate you!' From childhood came hidden anger and hurt provoked by the babysitter.

A week later

I had never seen Monie smile like that before. She described making friends. And she actually laughed. It was not the sort of laughter that I'd always known, which sounded crazy. The laughter was balanced and joyful. A dimple appeared on her cheek. I said to her, 'I've never heard you laugh like that before.'

She said, 'When I was able to think the terrible thought, then I was able to laugh.' She asked, 'How do I contend with people who are smarter than me?' She mentioned that she didn't know much about football.

I said there were people, probably hundreds of thousands, who were smarter at football than I was. I asked her who was smarter than her in her field. She listed a few notables. I said there was someone who was smarter in my field than I was.

'What do you do with that?' she asked.

I said, 'I learn from him.' I mentioned that probably all the taxi drivers in New York were smarter at being New York taxi drivers than I am.

'Does that mean everyone is good?' she asked.

'It means everyone is OK,' I said.

'I'm OK. You're OK,' she said.

I lay down on the floor and said, 'When you talk to me like that, then I can relax and not worry about you.'

'I can figure these things out myself,' she said.

Some time earlier she had moved to a bench at the far end of the room. I wondered about this new space between us. She was separating herself. And she had started to talk again about discharge.

Two weeks later

Monie talked of her discovery that she was OK. She spoke about taking responsibility and making decisions about her life.

Three weeks later

Monie wept over world peace. I watched her hands. She was digging into a mark on her finger that had had a scab. I asked her what she was doing. She replied: 'I am taking care of myself.' Soon her chatter reverted to more usual topics: her own inadequacy, everyone else's success. She was stroking the backs of her hands. Again the message was: 'I am taking care of myself.' Then the pattern was repeated, and her mind was caught up in her conviction that she was just no good. Each time self-denigration took over her mind, her body was proclaiming the opposite. It was saying, 'I care for myself.' It was offering her a chance to focus on something other than her negative thoughts – in short, to experience Self.

Three weeks later

Monie had left the residential facility for a few days. She had indicated that she wanted to talk face to face to the person she was still in love with, although she knew that he was not in love with her. I suggested that she call him before setting out for his home. She agreed to do so despite her insistence earlier in the day that she would set out to see him unannounced. I found out later that when she reached him by phone he had no wish to see her.

Her mind was set upon leaving the facility. She had been there the maximum permissible amount of time. She had started to move away from me as a therapist, and in recent weeks she had spoken of her fellow clients with a sense of distance and separation.

What had she gained from the experience, and what would she take away with her?

All concerned believed that she had made some progress with her anger. When she first arrived she was sullen and would have frequent angry outbursts. She also kept to herself. In recent weeks and months she had become in touch with her feelings. She was more centered. Two months before I had felt that the time had come for her placement in another facility, and just a fortnight before I had laid the groundwork for her transfer.

Would she survive the upheaval of possibly not having a place to stay? Would she perhaps contact a relative and stay with him or her? Would she be able to retain what she had gained and apply it to a new phase of her life, which could be more creative for her than previous ones? I trusted this would happen and that she would not come to harm. I hoped she would remember the times when she made contact with her Self.

Two weeks later

Monie said she had had a dream the night before. The person with whom she had been in love was in the water and couldn't swim the last lap. A tall, statuesque brunette with a red ribbon around her pony tail had gone in and brought her boyfriend to shore and cared for him. Monie said she realized she couldn't care for him as the other woman had. She had woken up feeling sad and had written a song.

I asked her if she would like to act out the dream. She made my co-therapist her boyfriend. I was to act out the part of the dark-haired woman.

As the dark-haired woman I said, 'I am at home in the water. The depths are known to me.' And I moved in a swimming motion around the room. I said, 'I have something you want.'

'*Yes*,' Monie said wholeheartedly and with amazement.

'What is it that I have?' I asked.

She said, 'Love.' It stopped me. She said that she had discussed with the psychiatrist her quick moves between love and hate. And this morning she had awakened with the thought it was not necessary for her to hate people any more.

Six days later

Monie expressed anger, and she cried. I tried to lead her back to the helpful figure in her dream. For a while I played the part, then I eased her into the role of the brunette. On leaving Monie said, 'I'm not sure where I stand, but the wise woman will help me.'

Monie's mother accompanied her back from a home visit that had taken place over Christmas. Her mother reached out to shake my hand on greeting me, and Monie did the same. The quality of that handshake was positive, assertive, childlike in its curiosity.

The two of them had brought some questions that they wished to discuss, among them the matter of Monie's plan for the future. I said I did not see her as always being in the mental health system – that is, living in a congregate care facility. I told the mother that I did not regard her daughter as schizophrenic. Later in the conversation Monie said to me, 'I've given up looking at myself in an unreal way – as a famous fashion designer and living with a certain young man.' She said it with tremendous pride and anticipation, as if something were over.

We agreed to do some planning over the coming months. She would take a college course. Maybe she could get some experience currently of being a waitress. She could get an apartment. She saw things as working out.

A month later

A few weeks ago, when Monie made her usual negative speech, I told her I was bored, not with her but with the speech. Last week I suggested that she get up and walk around the room where we met. As she walked she swung her arms and talked about her plans, such as learning to scuba dive after she had learned to swim. I couldn't fail to notice that she seemed centered. She said that she wondered if she really could base all her hopes on one person, as she had on the clothes designer: maybe she would have to find hope in herself rather than in anyone else. She said it had been 'shattering' when the man had not lived up to her expectations. She wondered if that had been the experience of her parents in divorce. She talked about how much she loved swimming, learning to swim. She had leaned back (arched her back) in the water, and that had been a wonderful experience. Those familiar with process-oriented psychology will understand. It is a pose that people often adopt in process-oriented work, and invariably they experience altered states of consciousness.

Two months later

Monie said, 'You have got me over my psychosis.'

With Monie's work I don't feel like drawing many conclusions. In our work together I followed a process. The process came out of her. The therapy followed that process through the bleak moments and returned many times to the ones when she laughed and there was joy. The process that was taking place was based upon growing acceptance of Self. It's hard to accept yourself when you've spent eighteen years in institutions; you are not like others on the outside, it seems. You don't have the things they have: apartments, cars, jobs, families, independence of move-ment. The savvy to operate in the world is one of the things that atrophies in institutions. Even when inner problems have been solved, at least to some extent, there is still that increasingly fast-moving world out there where you need not only a job but skills – those of an accountant to handle personal finances, those of a manager for household tasks and so on.

In our work together, which took place during a short hour every other week on average, we didn't get as far as developing coping skills. Some programs focus only on those. For a person with such low self-esteem as Monie had, skills training by itself would have been useless in the early stages. Someone who doesn't feel she 'can' in effect 'can't.'

Where is she now? She is at home with her mother in a Mid-western state. The work, which was allowing her process to unfold, added a dimension of Self to her experience.

It is important to add some further notes for the clinician. There are many ways to look at Monie. I choose to see her as having been caught in profound negativity. Negativity was her primary process. She clung to the idea of being loved by a fashion designer and being famous with him. Her desire to be loved by another creative person and to make trend-setting fashion with him caused her to disregard all the signals around her and to respond foolishly to unrequited love. Although she was in a negative state when I first knew her, still she clung to the idea that one day there would be the big pay-off and she would have her lover and fame. She identified getting over that idea with getting over her psychosis.

Her negativity ended after she contacted the forbidden image, the intolerable thought: childhood sexual abuse. This possibility was first touched off by following a channel switch from verbal–auditory (in her case, full of negativity) to proprioceptive. I asked my colleague to amplify the signal by placing her elbows and weight where Monie had said there was a load on her shoulders.

It took a long time and some bi-weekly meetings in which

some form of the dreaming body process was followed before she could come back to that dreaded experience. The day it actually came out I followed her statement 'I don't trust myself' (verbal –auditory). It led to 'hurt', and from there she located it in her body. Following this channel switch led to the buried experience. When she was about to block I acted her out as a child on the beach; she then switched to the visual channel. I lay on the beach, as she would have done. The rest of the experience came flooding before her eyes. She was actually seeing again what she had experienced at four years old and what she had barred from her awareness all that time.

Over the long period during which we worked together Monie had gathered strength, and many of the qualities that were part of her secondary process had started to express themselves. For example, my colleague said that about this time Monie had shown more love for the others than any of the other clients in the facility. We had established an iron trust. Awareness had grown in her. These qualities prevailed when she went to her would-be lover and found that he would not have her. She was able to give up love fixated to that individual, or image, as she had discovered it in herself and between herself and others. The wise woman in her (the brunette in her dream) took care of the ailing masculine figure, the spirit image in herself whom she loved. And Monie began to recognize in herself feminine wisdom and strength, both through kinesthesia (swimming) and through a blend of kinesthesia and proprioception in the arching of her back.

One can't give up something unless there is something to replace it. It seemed that in her process Monie had found something adequate to replace her fixated image of love, so that when the time came for it to go the groundwork was there for an experience of Self.

6 • Albert

I can still see his raging red hair and bright, reddened eyes. I made volumes of notes. There were eight hours of videotape. My co-therapist (a different woman from the one who had worked with Rose and Monie) gave a great deal to Albert in caring and managing his work periods. The other staff at the facility did not like him.

Describing my work with Albert is not going to be easy. Albert was like a storm; to interact placed one in a whirlwind. There were so many other clients. Why give this one so much attention? a colleague had asked me. To me the stakes seemed high. He told me later in our relationship what he had cost the state – the figures were over $10 million. He had been behind bars, chased by the police, washed (but not cleaned, I'm sure he would add) by the mental health system like some garment passing in and out of wringers. He upset everyone.

There were times when I really loved him. By taping together dozens of boxes and painting them, he created out of his institutional room a mass of slots. Then, using an old door, he fabricated a large table, high above the floor, where he could design things. He turned out five or six ideas an hour. And he did not need sleep as you and I do: a brief report of his activities would include more than most people could encompass in a busy day.

His reports were not always brief. One word to him could trigger a discourse. He liked this; when he was talking to me he was enjoying himself, and yet he also seemed to be under some obligation to fill out a project, to complete the job. He said that one of the reasons why he sometimes stayed up most of the night was that he felt that if he didn't do a particular job then, and the ones that followed, he might never get back to them.

He came to the facility from jail. A psychologist colleague

67

warned me about him. She said, 'He shows characterological qualities' ('antisocial' in the most recent jargon). Yet what unfolded is almost beyond belief. He has told me, 'I can now see that something can come out of my life within my lifetime.' In effect he was saying, for the first time, 'I can have a life.' He had never spoken this way before.

I had known Albert for about four months. I came into the picture because he was not working out in the workshop part of the program. This is not my department, but it is a requirement of all clients that they participate in the workshops. There were endless conflicts between Albert and the staff of the workshops. Things had come to an impasse. There was strong feeling that he should be asked to leave the program because of his behavior in the workshops, his 'difficult nature' and his insulting statements, which antagonized those who had to work with him. I said I would work with him for four weeks. During that time he would do workshop work with one of the head counselors in the clinical department.

Representatives of all the departments were present. He and one of the department heads were at loggerheads during the meeting. I watched him as he spoke. He was over-reactive. He could hardly sit still in his chair. Yet he did take a hint from me when I tried to mediate, and he sat back for a short time while the plan for the next month was proposed. He declared that his goal was to repair the dysfunctional parts of himself.

We were using videotape. One of his first statements was 'Paranoia is an offshoot of defensive thinking.' There is an option for the therapist: to accept a client's statement as it is until such a time that overwhelming experience argues against it or to assume that one 'knows' and to translate what people say into something else. I could have interpreted his statement as paranoia, but I chose not to do that: it was the paranoid element that modified his more basic defensive thinking, not the reverse. I decided to stick to his words, just as I attempt to stick to an image when I am working on a dream, rather than make incursions and detours into interpretations and seemingly related items.

He was defensive, that I knew. Everything about the first

sessions suggested it. He didn't allow me to talk: my remarks were rebuffed and dismissed. Some of his statements to me were directly to the point. He spoke of my seeking acceptance and reassurance from him.

He had had pneumococcal meningitis three years before. I noted that he was rubbing one of his knee joints and grimacing. 'Let's work with the problem of hurting,' I suggested.

He said, 'I don't like to be touched. Stay away or my reaction will be more violent.' He added, 'I had no idea you were contemplating moving in my circle.' He spoke of 'intelligent hostility'.

Before the session I had thought, I need to get him in the body. He is so defensive in the head that he will always win, so to speak, and we'll never get anywhere.

He spoke of people throwing rocks at him as a kid. He had scars on the back of his head. He said, 'We live in a very hostile environment.' He spoke of his burglaries and his knees (and feet) came straight up off the floor. He said, 'They wrote me up in other institutions as crazy.' There was pain in his joints. He poked his finger into the soft area behind his bent knee. He grimaced. He said, 'You wouldn't like it. I was tied down in chairs.'

He said his thumb used to tremble. He called this pre-Parkinsonian. He told me, 'You are thinking you have the control' (over that session). 'It is interaction, not control,' he stated, 'that is necessary for the gifted.'

He spoke of medications that he had been given at different times during his lifetime. He had taken Darvon in his early twenties, then codeine for a time. He didn't wear shirts or long pants because the cloth irritated his skin unbearably. 'But, oh, the *knees*. They are the worst.' He said, 'We gifted . . . Get out of our way . . . You're crippling us.'

What was I to make of all this?

I saw him putting people off with his talk of hyperactives and the gifted and his overt disgust for 'normals' like me, which he kept telling me about. Was I to see this talk of hyperactivity and being gifted as a giant defense?

My questions to him concerned my right, and his permission,

to treat his body. He told me to go away. He blocked verbal discussion. He bounced in his chair. He made a few choice remarks that were insulting and left me wondering a little about myself. I was unsure about whether to amplify his body gestures. He had told me directly to stay away.

He said, 'I am tired most of the time.' He spoke of being exhausted, and he bent over at the gut. He rocked as if hit. 'Hypers,' he said, 'see things others don't see.' He smiled. 'If I get you angry, then I am happy as a duck. I try to make it unpleasant for people to stop [them] saying what I don't want to hear. By this I attempt to orchestrate the responsiveness of the person I'm speaking to.'

He said that a major problem was to avoid hitting his knees – for example, on a drawer or ledge. He said 'thalmic rage' would result if his knees were interfered with. At the close of the session he said he was feeling worse in the legs. There was a grating inside the knee (his proprioceptive channel). I had called attention to his pain. I had thereby amplified his body processes. I asked him to go away and draw what was inside that knee.

In the session he had discussed the three ages of man. According to him, the first phase was the 'autonomous' phase. That was followed by the 'productive' stage of maturity. In the third phase 'a man is capable of being judged'. It was the old man on the mountain, the spiritual phase. Tentatively he told me of his embarking now on the productive stage of maturity. He was forty-one. All this indicated to me where he saw himself developmentally.

Two weeks later

Towards the end of the first hour Albert said something about his right leg being dead. I placed pillows over the leg, some below the knee and some above. There was a click or spasm. He said, 'That's interesting.' Then he mentioned that he had thought of taking an axe and cutting off the leg. 'That would kill the hyperactivity,' he said.

'How would that be?'

'I'd be on crutches,' he said.

'Shall we try that?' I asked.

The session took flight. Albert looked at the crutches I had supplied and said, 'Oh,' with the sound of pain. It was in his shoulders. Then he took the crutches and started walking with them. The role was so real that he said, 'What leg?' when I referred to the leg that was supposed to be missing. He also spoke of the phantom feeling of a missing limb as more real than the feeling of having a leg there.

'How is it different to walk on crutches?' I asked.

'You have to plan. Yeah, plan where you are going to move,' he explained. 'You have to take more account of your environment. Might cause an accident.' He sat down again.

'Why are you sitting down?'

'It hurts my shoulders.'

'You're tired.'

'I am tired.'

'But you are not supposed to get tired.' I was supporting his primary process, the one he identified with, in order to bring out his secondary process, which contained the opposite: the ambiguities, the less aware, creative possibilities for experimentation and change.

'I *do* get tired. I was tired this weekend . . . when I was nine years old we were at school on an island. The boys were going to climb up a mountain on the island. I ran on ahead to rest, and I would drink pop or coffee. Then I would start that again when the others arrived, running ahead and then resting for fear . . .'

'You would dart ahead and rest for fear . . .'

'Yeah, for fear I wouldn't reach the top. I couldn't have done it any other way. That's how a hyperactive does it, in sprints.'

That was the paradigm myth of Albert's life. It contained the basic picture of how he related to his energy. Everything else followed from that. In some of Arnold Mindell's seminars he works with the relation between childhood dreams or experiences and physical symptoms that have persisted in a person's life. Here that connection could be seen very clearly. Albert had a profound dislike of resting, being tired, being arthritic, crippled. By taking over his primary process and saying, 'You are not

71

supposed to get tired,' I amplified it, and the true myth of his life burst out, almost in flames.

Two weeks later

A week had passed since the last session of the four weeks of therapy that had been agreed upon. Albert was to appear before the committee of staff from several departments who would determine if he could work in the sheltered workshop program and, indeed, remain at the facility as a client.

I described to the committee something of the work we had done together. I said that he had dominated the first two sessions by talking. I found out eventually that he saw the opportunity of working in front of a video camera as his opportunity to tell his story to others who might view the tapes later. He was enormously self-protected. In the third session I provoked him somewhat. At one point he stood up and made some quick movements. No sooner had he started than he winced with pain. 'Oh, Christ,' he yelled as his knees locked into place. The pain in those knee joints had been apparent in the first session. I tried to stick with it and follow it. He returned to his chair. It obviously flustered him to have my attention drawn to what he was feeling in his joints, the proprioceptive channel. Yet there was a difference when he came back to the the second hour of the third session. He was interested in his reaction, which had taken him outside his conscious control. It had happened *to him*. It was an experience.

When he returned to his fourth session one week later he remarked, sardonically, that I had caused him a lot of pain. It would take three months to repress it again. 'Mind over matter,' he said in a shrill tone. He laughed. 'No matter . . . Ha, ha, ha.' He was rejecting the message.

The fourth session, however, contrasted with all the previous sessions. He was there to talk about a dream he had shared with very few people. It was a dream to help his own kind, hyperactives. He was calm. His manner was designed to win cooperation from others who, he perceived, could help in his cause. He would not work on himself – his own bodily process, that is – any more in that last session.

Now, as he met the committee, he said he experienced 25 to 30 per cent less pain. He said that formerly he would have bulled his way through any pain or tiredness. He reported that he had been to the staff physician and had received treatment in the form of medication.

I wondered whether there was a connection between the unacknowledged proprioceptive pain that had been reduced and his aggressive, self-protective stance towards the world, which had moved a little in the direction of socialization. I had to admit there was a connection.

Albert was allowed by the committee to remain at the institution.

Three weeks later

Statements made by Albert lately: 'I have to defend myself against them'; 'Now I can become vicious tomorrow'; 'You're known by the enemies you keep excited.'

Three weeks later

Albert had come to my office the evening before. He had been in a state. His relationship with his work supervisor within the facility had come dangerously close to terminating. He wanted to leave the facility for a few days to write a description of himself for all other staff. I saw this as an enormous effort on his part to defend himself, and I told him so. I was aware of the time (my wife was waiting for me outside) but not the timing. I saw the problem in him, saw him as the problem; that was easier and quicker for me, as I couldn't see the supervisor changing his position. The structure did not support such action, even if Albert bore the greater part of the onus for the rift. And he was making me uncomfortable by describing me as Archimedes-like. I rejected this tribute, perhaps partly because it was attractive. I offered to meet him and his supervisor, and we left it that way. As he left my office he looked hurt and misunderstood. The next day he was hopping up and down in his chair. Some of his references were grandiose. However, when he came to the point of describing me, he was right. He referred to me as a sunny-day patriot. The British would have to burn down my house before I went to war. I had to agree with him inwardly.

I remarked that he wasn't holding my gaze and that he was angry with me, at which he pulled away. But I kept him to the topic. I told him that I didn't have a fixed idea of him; sometimes he was brilliant and sometimes he was off the wall. He concurred. I said that in a place such as the facility he didn't need to define himself because the staff were trained in instances such as his to throw a net over the patient. The more he protested, the more his diagnosis would be confirmed in people's minds.

I had done some more thinking, but this time I didn't burden him with my thoughts. He lacked social interest, according to Adler's work. If he could just get along with one person, then he would not need to define himself at all. But hadn't he said that he had concluded he had problems working with people? People weren't his marketplace, so to speak. It wasn't necessary to bring up that point in a flat-footed fashion.

Instead I told him I cared about him, that I had thought about him many times during the weekend when I was meditating. Was I seeing a part of myself in him? Or did I really care for him? The latter, I think. I explained that I knew this was not his territory – feeling. But when he left he expressed himself by coming over to me and putting his hand on my shoulder.

There was a change. I was certainly different. I saw him differently too. He had my blessing to write this 'definition' of himself.

He stated that since coming to the facility his position had changed: he was no longer threatened – he was now being challenged.

He came back later in the day. He said it would be some time before he could be what I wanted him to be, mind and feeling. He wouldn't allow that for himself until he had established a foundation for hyperactive kids.

It was the relationship channel that was being used in Albert's therapy.

There was one other person who liked him at the facility. She was my co-therapist. It had not always been so. He had come to me once complaining of her; I had simply given him the suggestion that he talk to her directly about his complaint. Instead of attacking I had suggested that he simply express what her action caused him to feel. She was open to him at that moment, and Albert found that he did not have to bully everyone and run right over them to get his way. This small incident came to him with the magnitude of revelation. It was almost as if he had grown up after a lifetime in the wild.

Three weeks later

Albert thought I was supporting him in his conflicts with other staff. I told him that fell within the Mother, his relation with her but not with me. He denied the value of the sessions we had had together. He seemed very angry.

We walked to my office. He said, 'Now you listen to me.'

I retorted, even more loudly and pointing my finger, 'Now you listen to *me*.' I explained to him that he needed me – if he ever wanted to get anything across about hyper kids. I could do the writing. He protested that I had not taken the time to watch the tapes of our four sessions together. I said that I had been so busy putting out fires, the negative interactions between himself and others, that I hadn't had time to do anything along those lines. Then I said, 'You stop the fires, and we'll start the tapes tomorrow.' We struck a deal. I knew I was manipulating him, even though my intention to follow through was genuine. But with a manipulative hyper, you have to be a bit of a trickster.

Four days later

It had been an interesting week. One afternoon we had worked
on the tapes of our earlier sessions. He explained some motions
and gestures. I listened and made notes. He seemed defensive in
the responses that he made. He spoke of my being able to help
him focus. He seemed to accept my direction to go for a 'strategy'
rather than using his energy indiscriminately. He spoke of doing
things out of affection for my co-therapist and me. I expressed
interest in his desire to do things for gifted and hyperactive
people. Once, when he saw me in the stairwell, he spoke of me
as a conscience.

That day he had been prescribed a stimulant for the central
nervous system. He said he was going to tell me something he
had never told anyone before. He was the Messiah. I asked him
what that meant. He said it was the 'cutting edge'. He envisaged
a new world run by 'hypers'.

I had the uneasy feeling that if I did not speak, I would be
aiding and abetting his fantasy. All I could do was to speak out
of myself. I told him that I didn't see a person who took such a
stance as living his or her life in the world as an individual. He
accepted this. I said that people like him seemed to be living out
of a pattern (born of the unconscious and contained in myth). I
could not help but think of something Marie-Louise von Franz
had said. She discusses how the shadow of the person in trouble
with the law can be the opposite, shadow bright in tone. She
writes: 'We know also that sometimes people who live their
darkest side and repress their better ego have all sorts of dreams
of Christ, redeemer of mankind . . .'[1] I had seen all along that
Albert's conceptions of himself were grandiose. At that point he
was vocationally dysfunctional and he had great problems in
getting along with people.

If we accept Jung's view of the unconscious as playing a
compensating role in conscious life, then clearly a notion of the
Messiah, in all its greatness, replaces lack of accomplishment in
reality. Also when the ego is weak its self-concept is too diminished to relate to unconscious process; in addition, the unconscious can simply fill the space. The larger-than-life figure takes

the place of the real person, who regards him- or herself as living less than the life of an ordinary person. Albert reacted by protesting that he was more – he was gifted, hyper. And when he really let his guard down, he declared that he was the Messiah.

'Tell him it is not so', some would have admonished. The view reflected by such advice would also possibly advise someone who weighed 300 lbs to lose all that weight. The view of process-oriented psychotherapy would be to understand the value and importance that such weight has for the individual, not to ask that person to give it up unless there was some new and more fulfilling direction for the energy.

I couldn't destroy Albert's delusion. I know what it is like to be caught in a pattern rather than live one's own life. When a pattern is a substitute for living, it can be used as an excuse for one's shortcomings; when one lives in relation to a pattern the 'I' is maintained in the modesty and good humor of the human plane while taking sustenance and inspiration at times from the 'not-I' of the great collective storehouse of gods and goddesses and other dynamic figures.[2]

Five days later

Albert came to my office to share with me a tape that recorded a conversation he had had with another client, John. There had been an incident in which Albert had been threatened by the hostile actions of yet another client. Afterwards John had written Albert a poem that reflected the solidarity he felt with him in the face of an unfair threat. Albert had been very taken by this gesture and had asked to interview John.

What stands out in the tape is Albert's interest, interviewing technique and even therapeutic touch. He seems like a really nice person.

When he came into my office to share this tape he spoke of modesty in relation to something greater than himself. I said I had felt the same thing in my work with him on at least one occasion. He said he was going to erase that from his mind. I asked him about it as he was leaving. He said, 'The model shouldn't take credit for the work of the artist.' I was sure he was referring to himself as the artist, as that would have been consistent with the concept of himself that he often expresses. Instead he said he wouldn't want to take any credit for the artistry of *my* work, that he was finding more confidence in himself (just as I was). I sensed a positive transference of some nascent quality in himself that he saw, or felt he saw, in me.

Five days later

'I am dysfunctional.'

'What is that?' I asked.

Albert didn't answer directly. He proposed an acid test for hyperactivity. He talked about going to a library. 'When I get excited I have to go get coffee or a coke. There is nothing that allowed me to function in the library. Ritalin and no meds interfered. Silert is helping. A massive shift in my behavior [is occurring]. Always before I had no faith that there would be a tomorrow. If you didn't get it done today, then you would never get back to it.' He said he would work thirty to forty hours in a row to get a task done. 'My ability to write quietly is brand-new.'

He said, 'If you do have a gifted child, or if you have had rough experiences in your life' – does he equate the two groups? Do they overlap? – 'the danger is that you might become arrogant.'

I reiterated his statement.

He spoke of a white crow. Having lived the antisocial side of himself (the black crow), he had another side to him that was highly moral, seen as the white crow. On some issues he was moral to a fault. It was an unadapted condition in him. He was not able to consider anything other than his true rights.

He spoke of guardians. He said, 'You and the co-therapist are our moral guardians.'

What I was learning from my work with him was that I should not over-react with anxiousness. Only if I didn't react thus could the process that was happening go on.

One week later

What I couldn't get over was this: deep within Albert was someone who could trust and share and care, but of all things he was most secretive of that. 'Take the tapes home,' he urged me. Could someone of good faith have been so hurt that, by all means possible, he had kept this side of himself hidden and repressed? There we had the meaning of his paranoid-like personality. I was touched and gratified that his trust in me had led to this revelation. Could it possibly be extended to others? Would this ethical quality and his caring for people find further outlets and eventually be able to come out of hiding?

Why was it so surprising that we should find human nature here?

Two days later

Albert mentioned that he had been to see the doctor about his knees. He said they were damaged. He then began to connect this damage with his hyperactivity. He said that even as a young person his knees had hurt, as he put it, from overactivity and speedy movements. He also mentioned that he had walked on the sides of his feet, which put his knees in a perilous position.

It was interesting to me that when this subject had arisen in our work together some four months before I had made the same connections, though I said nothing to him. The process had been moving along at a very rapid pace, which he was determining. I'd felt that my interpretation did not belong in the process at that point. Now he had integrated the connection between his hurting knees and his energy cycle. He said the doctor had given him some gentle exercises for strengthening his knees. He had started to write. He was trying to define hyperactivity. Only then would we know, he said, what the treatment should be. The library, as he had stated, was one of the most difficult territories for him. Now he was working on that aspect of what he called his 'dysfunction'.

I got the feeling that the process was carrying him – that is, things were moving inside him rather than under my direction. He was working on the pain, which led him back to his energy cycle.

Staff had begun to notice a change in him. He did not antagonize people any more. He was beginning to get his needs met.

What about the fact that the major body work done with Albert was only coming up directly in his awareness then? It had not been integrated quickly. Also, it had not been followed by other body work. Perhaps Albert's defensiveness about offering himself to body work at all partly accounted for the four-month period of integration; his proprioceptive channel was one of his less accessible channels and therefore more unconscious. His primary process was activity, even over-activity. His secondary process was pain in the joints, especially the knees. Theoretically too acknowledgment of pain in the muscles, tissues and joints was the opposite of his philosophy, 'I must keep on, whatever the consequences.'

The work had come round full circle. His acknowledgment of pain, to the extent of discussing it with the physician, was a step towards his integration. He was ceasing to suppress his body processes, an instinct so long in force in his life and so vital to the maintenance of his one-sided system of behavior – that is, being active whether appropriate or not.

This came at a time when the unit staff reported that he was calmer. When he started to listen more to his body he became less hyperactive. When he started to work directly on the dysfunction of his hyperactivity, through writing and considering the use of a library, his hyperactivity was less 'lived'; it was being related to instead.

Later that week

Hyperactive people make everything happen. They ferret out conflicts, anomalies, lack of definition. This is their specialty – to find the one moral point where there may be the misappropriation of a personal right. If they are aggrieved, they will hang on to the bitter end.

Albert came to my door and said he could not be sure about his awareness of his own actions.

The next day

Albert said our recent talks had changed everything. He said his negativity with regard to the facility had disappeared.

A week later

Albert was beginning to realize what had been happening at each point during his conflicts with staff. He was learning about himself. He was trying new alternatives. Instead of reacting instantly with anger, he was going off to write things down and then coming back to talk with people. Meanwhile he was saying to himself, 'Aha, I am reacting *that* way. What does it mean? David said, "Try it."'

'I rejected it out of hand,' he reported. 'Then a little later I tried it. I could not react impulsively at the moment. I could talk with people later. That was the new option.'

He really did want a program for the gifted. When he was talking I became aware that some sudden leap of perception was needed to apprehend what was going on in him when he was in a state of clarity and was not talking about trivia: a giant screen, so to speak, was all that I could think of. English is limited. Verbal, linear thought is limited. To apprehend him, something bigger, more comprehensive in content and immediacy, was needed.

He was gifted, not just hyperactive. This was the first time I would have said that.

He said, 'You can bring a skunk to a veterinarian and tell him to treat it. He will. But it is still a skunk.'

He also said that he operated from a philosophy of morality. Change that philosophy and the behavior changed. It was like moving a switch on the railroad, so that the engine and all the cars (behavior) went down another track.

Three months later

Listening to his body connected Albert with his energy pattern. He began to put the hurting knees and the hyperactivity together. He did this himself. At the same time he listened more to himself, took up writing, showed small signs of consciousness, awareness, trust in me.

The principles of his treatment were these:

1. picturing two vents: the energy could flow through either the positive vent or the negative one;
2. using energy to promote the opening of the positive vent – that is the choice of therapy and therapists;
3. keeping the concept of the moral shadow pivotal: what was unconscious in our law-breaker Albert was less developed and very moral. It needed further development. It was his secondary process to be moral.

How do we view the client? Mindell formulates that there are basically two ways: what people do should be different; what people do is somehow right.

How do we view therapy? We give people new experiences. The new experiences grow out of working directly with the body and with what people are experiencing. The new experiences reorganize the energy of the body.

We don't give the new experiences. The experiences come from following the process.

About a week later

Two very dramatic things happened before Albert left the program. The first concerned his plans to bring a suit against one of the top administrators of the institution because some of his possessions had been packed up in his absence. At that time almost every one of my colleagues had turned against him, some for his insolent behavior. Again I was having to put out brush fires. I called my co-therapist into my office with him.

I took a number of things out of my desk – Sellotape dispenser, desk-light clamp, small board, large paperclip, about twenty items in all. With each I made a trip over to one of the vacant chairs in my office. On another vacant chair, at the opposite side of the room, I placed a book entitled *The Drama of the Gifted Child*[3] and the videotapes we had made together.

Referring to his dream about doing something for hyperactive persons, I said, 'We can do either *this* or *this*. We can't do both.' All my feeling went into it. It was a crossroads for him. I tolerated no interruptions or moving away from the point. A few hours later he came back and said he had decided to drop the suit.

One week later Albert was asked to leave the program. He had fallen in love with another client and had tried to reach her at night by going through the staff station. When I talked with him that afternoon, I said, 'You don't have to go back to jail.' He seemed intent upon doing just that.

Later he returned. He said he would get an apartment. He said, 'I thought you would want me to do something positive.'

I remain in awe of Albert's capacity to change so much – as he put it, to pull the railroad switch and make all the cars go down another track. For a short time in that protected environment he experienced his secondary process, that of being a moral person, in his *actions*. Whenever he explored that morality in a highly structured way we saw another side of Albert. In Taoism a person is sometimes one thing and then the opposite. In Albert the opposites were very far apart. Awareness, the key, was the newcomer to the scene. Did this emerge because we prompted him to notice the pain in his joints, which connected him with his body and maybe his feelings, and let him experience the other side of his hyperactivity?

Albert was a bone of contention between me and other members of staff, who thought that to give him time and to work seriously with him was an error of judgment and unprofessional. Since I held a key position, this began to make everyone feel uncomfortable. I wanted to arrange a staff session in which I could explain my treatment plan, but, alas, Albert was kicked out the morning before that could take place.

It was a great pity that we could not use the conflict-resolution approach of process-oriented psychology. If we had, perhaps the staff, all of us, could have avoided becoming personally identified with any one approach or stance, either pro- or anti-Albert. The depersonalization of conflict, which allows people to adopt less rigid and dogmatic positions, can open up the way to a broader range of feelings and opinions.

Albert wanted to get rid of his dreambody knees. In his fantasy they were causing him all his problems: his hyperactivity, his aching tiredness, his hurt. He recognized that it was his dreambody knees that mattered, that needed treatment, because cutting off his real legs would still leave him with his phantom knees.

Although the dreambody appears to move around in people, to represent itself in different perceptual systems and different locations of the same channel (Albert's shoulders ached when he saw the crutches), in our first two sessions it was his knees that seemed to signal nearly everything about his situation and condition. His knees were his dreambody talking to him. They didn't want to be touched; they were hypersensitive. He protected (defended) them at all costs. Memories of burglaries made his knees lift. When he spoke of his hurt he remembered being called crazy in other institutions. His overall reaction to the un-understanding public and professionals (normals) was that they were crippling him. The dreambody was being crippled through his interactions with society.

Why did this process work for Albert? The shift of channels was from verbal–auditory, where he was stuck, defended, to proprioception. We followed the signal. It opened the door for the dreambody to express itself. Four months went by before he acknowledged that this was the key that awakened the Self. It was the seed of awareness. It was his body dreaming.

The dream appeared in the story of his running ahead of the other boys up the hill for fear he wouldn't be able to make it. This dream was occurring in his knees. When he imagined he didn't have a real leg the phantom leg, the dreambody, told him he was going to have to take more account of his environment.

When the four weeks of therapy were concluded we began to relate; we entered the relationship channel. The point of contact in proprioception allowed the relationship to be established. The channels shifted again. In the relationship channel I picked up messages about my own shortcomings. Albert started to gain something from me: I was protecting his morality.

In the relationship channel he started to become what he imagined existed in me. He wanted to do what he thought I would approve of – in his words, to live positive action. We began to share a dream. It was to collaborate in a project that would improve the lot of 'hypers' (and the hyper in him). A chapter of my book would be about him, I told him. He wanted to help me with a word processor for typing the manuscript.

Behind the dream is enormous potential for the gifted individual. The dreaming body is trying to get us there, even if, in Albert's case, it must express itself within the confines of institutions and jails. That has a lot to do with the way our society looks on these things. The next part of the book begins with the *creative*, a term that I would like to see applied to many of the wounded, Albert and Rose being prime examples.

When the dreambody becomes as active and sometimes destructive, as it was in Albert's case (when he missed the signals), it must be expelled or imprisoned, as logic dictates. When treated by means of following channel switches, amplifying and using the bond of human love, the possibility exists for the dreambody to realize its perspective in the world. In Albert's fantasy that meant the possible creation of a place for 'hypers'. Looked at analytically, it could also mean that society as a whole could grow to the understanding that an Albert exists in many of us and therefore deserves a place in our individual and collective awareness. As long as this is not the case, the division will remain absolute in some people's minds. And the dreambody will again be imprisoned, not only in Albert but also in ourselves.

PART THREE

·

Working with the Creative

7 • *Four People on a Spiritual Journey*

I went on a trip to Greece with four architects. I am dependent on their experiences. They left me their notes.

It may be asked what the connection is between these four characters and those described earlier in the book. The spirit is such that it needs lifting. It can be lifted among those who have been in a terrible darkness, and it can be lifted among those who are not in such pain. It is important always to have balance (the god Apollo) in one's life, in the people one meets, even in a book.

My four friends who went with me to Greece provided great balance for me in my work with the chronically mentally ill. Here is a brief story of four people responding to the light on a different plane from that of the people we met in earlier chapters. Working with process is applicable in both spheres.

They were in the airport bus that fetches travellers from planes. The Athens terminal shone almost like midday in the evening sun. Aristotle, one of the four American architects, was saying loudly, 'But I *am* Greek!'

A few minutes before he had told his friends a dream he had had just before coming to Greece. In the dream he had said, 'I am Greek,' and an old man had challenged him; he had said, 'You don't speak Greek, you are not second-generation Greek-American and your family are no longer Orthodox.' Aristotle stood up (this is when his voice started to get loud in the bus), and he repeated, staring the old man down, 'I *am* Greek!'

But Aristotle had his doubts too. The river of noise outside his hotel window intensified his fears. What if he couldn't sleep? Reading *Zorba the Greek* in his bed at 2.30 a.m. was no comfort. Would his earache get worse? Would he be able to find a doctor in the little town where he was going? It was strange, he thought, to come to Greece looking for his spiritual heritage. What was even stranger, he thought, as his misgivings really took hold of him, was that he should conceive of such a search as one that could be synchronistic with the search of some in the monastic communities who were looking to early Greek Christianity from a spiritually bereft West. He didn't know if he could stand not being able to go to sleep. The noise of the people below, the cacophony of muffler-less mopeds, reminded him of sounds cascading off canyon walls, a deep and desperate noise, inviting a desperate plunge. He decided to process the slight tremble in his hands, working on himself in a process way. His motions became stronger and bigger. Then he was walking. He couldn't let down his anima by giving up on his vision.

In his sleep a dream developed. A tear formed of the love between himself and his wife. Light went into it; it turned into a diamond, indestructible. His deep sleep, although short, was like hours. And during this sleep appeared a powerful spiritual figure from Greece itself, a man in gold robes, a monk, carved out of Greek rock, strong, able to hold his spirituality with his powerful torso. He was giving something to Aristotle, as Aristotle later told us. It was a miracle: he took up residence in Aristotle's body. The torque of all this old man's power formed itself in Aristotle's legs and pelvis.

Homer was one of those solid Americans whose family has been on the North American continent long enough for him to carry his body without apology – a man whose suits were worn but of the finest quality. Homer knew Jean-Paul Sartre and Graham Greene and had been to parties with T. S. Eliot. He was studying Greek. He knew more about Greece than any of the others, although he had no particular connection with the country. In fact, his nose, with its hazardous bend, identified him as a member of an Ayrshire clan.

He told the others that Jung had told him that what was special about the Greeks among all Westerners was that they had never had a Reformation. The Greeks were still in touch with all the gods, all the instincts. There was no radical break between the mind and the patterns that had governed and guided human life through the centuries.

One evening Homer met Zorba. He described the experience to us. He read us the letter he was sending home.

> Last night was a really unbelievable experience. You know how those things happen sometimes. Greece was playing Russia for the *finals* in basketball. When Greece won all the Greeks went really crazy mad. You can't imagine the noise, everyone honking the horn. The streets filled. Cars driving absolutely wild. I met a couple of black Canadians in my hotel and suggested we go to the Plaka. We came outside our hotel on a very busy city artery from the stadium. The crowd had just broken loose. I got a cab just as he was pulling out. Yes, he would take us to the Plaka, about four kilometers away. Horns blowing. He was wild, screaming, 'Greece is NUMBER ONE!' Then he said, 'You won't be able to get back from the Plaka tonight because *all the taxes will go on vacation.*' He said, 'I will get you back.' It was one of those wild generous things. I said, 'We don't have much money.' It turned out he charged about the regular price. But no one else was working. On the avenue as we were returning from the Plaka, I noticed that everyone was walking, no taxes.
>
> I got to experience Greece when it was wild, ecstatic.

The Athenians like to spend their time at Syntagma Square. Foreigners gather there, sitting at the small tables with glasses of water and small glasses of ouzo. You can even go there at ten in the morning. It was about then that Homer suggested that Phil do just that one morning, when the four architects and I had had a late breakfast. Phil was nervously twitching his cigarette and asking Homer if he should take a flight to Crete for the weekend or hire a car, take in Sounion and return to Athens for another long night in the Plaka. Homer said, 'Just go sit and have a coffee in Syntagma Square.'

Phil told us later that no sooner had he sat down than he saw an old friend of his from Detroit, and the friend said he and his young wife were going to Delphi. They asked Phil to come along. They had a warm time together. Phil later received a letter from his friends while we were still in Greece. They sent this:

Conceived at Delphi

They stole away to Delphi. The couple stayed
where rocks are reaching out to touch the air
and gods would play if gods did anywhere.
Their bed on the lip of infinity was laid,
and drunk with sky, they clove to mortal frame.
In such a fold a civilization could fare
forth; in such a fold our earthly pair
conceived a child above the olive plain.
Lie peaceful, little babe, in mother's fold.
Then later when down lies dark upon your face
and stones are dreamt like those, may you be told –
should you be led, this reliquary to trace –
they stole away to Delphi. What vapors rolled,
what tale of destiny in this moment embrace?

It was late one evening in the Plaka. The four had found a
taverna (restaurant) towards the end of the Plaka in the
direction of the Agora and the modern flea market. In the
restaurant there was only one Greek family and a few old Greek
men. The family, which was poor to judge by outward appear-
ances, was celebrating a betrothal. Young and old danced. The
plates were smashed on the floor (perhaps at home they would
have had such a set for a lifetime). The three *bouzouki* players
might have looked tired by some standards – at least they had
not achieved their dream to be famous. But there was a glow
about their eyes when they saw you. It was like the thousand-
fingered dance they mastered in order to accompany an evening
during which warm breezes and the sparkle around old men's
feet dancing met to still the moment in which otherwise bliss
might have gone unheeded.

That special evening, in the taverna under the stars, Aristotle
lost his reluctance. He had never believed in rebirth, he said. He
said he had thought there were a lot of good things about Eastern
religions, but he could never appreciate reincarnation. Then one
night he had a dream.

In the dream a finger went to a map of Greece, and the voice
of the dream said, 'You were here.' It was east of Thessalonika,
between Thessalonika and Istanbul. It was just above the sea on

the map. Then he began to see. There was a small house with white interior walls. A soldier of the Roman army was passing on. He was a Christian. It seemed about the fourth century, Aristotle said. Aristotle wouldn't tell us the rest of the dream except to say it was filled with a sense of resurrection.

'Oh, everybody thinks he or she was important in some previous life,' chimed in Phil, who was starting to reel after several Scotches.

'That may be,' Aristotle admitted, 'but hear the rest of the dream.'

The finger went to the other side of the map of Greece, north again but this time just south of Albania. Again the voice said, 'You were here,' pointing to a taverna like the plain ones near the square in Nafplion.

And Aristotle saw a man with an ordinary calling in life having a good time. 'This must have been about the nineteenth century,' he said.

Esther, the one woman with us, wrote of Aristotle's experience:

> Into this man's dying hour he peered,
> soldier he'd lived, leader in legionaires of Rome –
> turned Christian, then in whitened chambers spread
> a bright and resurrecting light about his complete home.

Aristotle had been the one who got them all to come to Greece, Phil said, 'and you mean it was to chase *that* rainbow?'

Aristotle said he felt he was risking a lot to pull all that material out in front of his friends. Homer didn't try to defend him. He just leaned over and placed his broad hand on Aristotle's shoulder.

'You remember Jung's dream?' Esther said. 'He dreamed he was on a journey, hiking in a hilly landscape; the sun shone and he saw in all directions.' Then she quoted Jung:

> I came to a small wayside chapel. The door was ajar, and I went in. To my surprise there was no image of the Virgin on the altar, and no crucifix either, but only a wonderful flower arrangement. But then I saw that on the floor in front of the altar, facing me sat a yogi – in lotus posture, in deep meditation. When I looked at him more closely I realized that he had my face. I started in profound fright, and

awoke with the thought: 'Aha, so he is the one who is meditating me. He has a dream, and I am it.' I knew that when he awakened, I would no longer be.[1]

Esther said that was part of what the rites at Eleusis were about.

Phil said, 'You mean that life seems to throw up the beautiful dark-eyed woman generation after generation, and over the dark course of history, and through persecution like the Turks here for four centuries?' He continued, 'And the woman I saw in the market today is like the one on the vase of the museum at the Agora! Long live the dark-eyed feminine,' he chanted as the four hopped and slid down the marble steps leading from the Plaka into the modern town and their hotel.

Esther wrote:

Greece

> I give my warmth to you
> I have plenty for my own
> Rest in my simple ease
> eat my ripened tomatoes
> dip bread in salad oil
> climb the olden steps
> rise to the heights and
> see my mountains beyond
> locate yourself in my landscape.[2]

The next day Aristotle was on his trail again. He found the small church dedicated to St Dimitrios, just in the shadow of the Acropolis on the hill known as Aereopagis. Aristotle shared the note from his journal:

At St Dimitrios

I was meditating on what it might mean that in a past life there had been a light throughout the house, of this being as he passed on, an enlightenment. I was working, working, working on the idea. Then I became aware of the blood on my hands. I almost went to sleep. A woman came in in white raiment. Then I saw the light increase inside . . . 'The freshness of the body': this phrase occurred to me. It was tied to the Resurrection and the experience of the energy field of another person a yard or so away.

This all took place, Aristotle said later, just in front of one of those dark, ancient icons, black with age and covered with silver.

A week later in another town near Patras

Aristotle saw Vasillis, a Greek fisherman whom he had met several days earlier. He was sitting alone in a café on the waterfront, where people stroll at night. He was drinking a beer. He looked dejected.

Aristotle listened to him and watched him. Aristotle said, 'I have met many wonderful people in this town but you have taught me the most.'

For a moment Vasillis looked as if he believed Aristotle. Then he lapsed into his sorrow. Vasillis asked, 'How can people laugh at me when I cry?' He told Aristotle that in his heart and in his head he hurt. He cried, 'I can't stand it any more.' He said he had lied when he had told Aristotle a few days earlier that he had a strong heart.

Aristotle told Vasillis that he wanted to tell him a story and asked him for an idea. 'What idea?' Vasillis asked.

'Any idea,' Aristotle said.

Vasillis reached over and touched Aristotle's shoulder. This gave Aristotle the idea he needed. He dreamed up a story to tell his friend because he sensed this was behind Vasillis' story. He said, 'There is a young boy. He always wants to please others with whom he has grown up, but whatever he does it never seems quite enough. The boy tries harder and harder because now he has an inner critic who will never rest. Then, when he is over forty, he meets a teacher who lets him strive harder and harder, moving about a room doing process work, and then the teacher grabs him and stops his striving. He and another process teacher pin him down so he cannot move. He can't so much as stretch his toes. When he is without all hope he feels a hand on his shoulder. It is enough. It is enough for him just to be himself.'

Aristotle had put the story together from fragments of people's lives he had known. It seemed right. Vasillis' demeanor had changed. Aristotle said, 'I will pray that the spirit protectors look after you.'

Vasillis replied, 'You have cleansed my heart.'

The next day, at breakfast, Homer said he had heard a gunshot and women's screams in the night. Then he asked, 'Could it have been . . . Vasillis?' Homer recalled the last meeting he had with him.

He had found Vasillis in the restaurant by the quay where he and Vasillis had come after their first meeting. Vasillis was depressed and was crying. He talked about how he had been teased by a few of the men in the town who just wouldn't let up on him.

Homer asked him to recall all the photos he had taken when Vasillis had shown him the town. Well, that very afternoon Homer had pushed the wrong switch on his camera and all the film had come tumbling out. As the roll spiraled to the floor, Homer took it up in his hands and played around with it like a friendly snake. Vasillis laughed throatily at the débâcle.

Esther said that she would help Homer to search for Vasillis that afternoon. Someone should be able to tell them, in spite of their limited Greek, what had happened to him. They all agreed to meet that night for supper at the taverna by the sea where all the local Greek fishermen go.

If Vasillis had died, Aristotle thought, it would mean that the simple Christian ethic was unworkable. Vasillis had said in one of their early talks, quoting Jesus, 'If you have two coats, and you meet a man who has none, then give him the one.' Vasillis spoke from the heart. Aristotle had said that this was one of the truest and most touching things that anyone had ever said to him.

Aristotle went back to his hotel. He fell asleep in the late morning. That night in the taverna he told the others what had happened. He said he had dreamed that all the pieces of the visit to Greece had been torn apart and were strewn over the floor. He rose from the dream deeply disturbed, and he decided to work on the dream. He tore a large white sheet of paper into eighteen ragged pieces. On these he wrote the things that had affected him about his journey to Greece:

breeze	bliss
the Monk	meanings
water	home
contentment	Greek music
helping	joy in meeting
fortune	hope
clean body	rest
pathways, rocky stairs	air
Vasillis	Light

He took the tattered fragments of paper and tossed them about the room. Then he bent down, laboriously gathered each piece from the floor and began the process of fitting the little edges together. Only after a very long period of tedious matching was he able to re-create the whole. He sighed.

Phil, who had so far been absent from the evening dinner gathering, suddenly appeared, his arm around a tired-looking Vasillis. They were all talking again, the four architects and Vasillis. Aristotle was writing on his napkin:

> You, too, are rocked by waves and sounds
> and the night reaches its fingers
> into your soul, never mind your religion
> the gods are waves, the goddess, night
>
> If you are blessed to meet a Greek
> a true Greek, then find one
> ready to share the comely nature
> these gods, goddesses give to us.
>
> It reaches you through his smile
> his enthusiastic sounds and eyes
> before you know it, you reach a place –
> no words, no thoughts, just music in the heart.

And before the four architects left Greece Aristotle wrote:

The capitol of the world
is where the heart is lovely
Flowers bloom there beside
narrow, rocky stairs
begonias red, hyacinths climbing.

No one wakes to thoughts
which disturbed the yesterday
Birds chatter instead
to greet the morning
with its proper hymn.

Why does he smile at me
Why, she, time to talk
The gods have given
everything here
I hear it in my humming.

8 • Chad: an Analysis with Poems as Markers

Truly Jung was one of 'spherical intelligence', as Henry Murray has said. It was because he allowed that spirit of intelligence to wander where few had gone that he is remembered today. He thought about problems and encountered forms of literature that his stuffier contemporaries would never have dared to consider in published articles.

Statements in his autobiography move beyond the simple perceptual world of positivist or behaviorist world views prevalent today. His intuition of life – he likened life to a rhizome, with imperceptible roots beneath the surface – is expressed in his voluminous, unfolding, imaginative prose, lucid and beautiful. He is the inspirer *par excellence* of the poet, of poetic experience and expression.

Jung and the artistic: you will remember the decisive point in Jung's life when he parted company with the anima who wanted him to think of himself as a great artist. Yet he was an artist. Perhaps the point to be made is this: Jung was an artist in whom the power of awareness was dominant. Each stroke of beauty is at the same time two steps forward into the awareness of what lies beneath art and life itself, the Great Creative unconscious or Self. As time goes on, perhaps he will inspire the union of psychological understanding and artistic expression in others.

I believe that such was Chad's experience of Jung. Chad was an analysand whom I saw intermittently over a twenty-year period. Poetry was his love, yet he had a fear of bringing it into the world. He did many different types of work during these years, but poetry was always there as a marker for his inner experience. It was the inner journey that was his real journey – or so it seemed for many years. As is often the case, that time of inner ripening for him was later balanced with a fruitfulness with respect to others. But let us start at the beginning of the story.

Chad's work began with a poem.

A Flame

May I upon the snows of death set glowing
a flame from now, past known and knowing
heated belief, and on three questions feeding
themselves the test if life be worth the leading:

Will my love be saying, 'I give you all,'
when leaves have dropped and she has given all?

Will the boy in me requite the blows of childhood years –
or construct a temple of his rebuffed fears?

Will that unrealizable line begin to rhyme?
. . . The hum of three logs burning to the end of time.

Chad's early adult life was preoccupied with children. Once he brought me a poem by his ten-year-old daughter. He read it to me.

> I was born on a hill
> the biggest hill
> I got so ill
> that I nearly died
> but once in my sleep
> I saw God
> he gave me life.

Chad lived in England for some time. He was intrigued by the fact that both T. S. Eliot and Robert Frost had spent time there – in Eliot's case, of course, the rest of his life. Chad's first experience of a Norfolk village is suggested in the following poem.

Sheltered Island Lands

Ebullient clouds were strewn in celestial tiers,
the inward stairs which reached the unspied dome
and gave a height unknown in other spheres
expanse to sheltered island lands, to home.
The pastures past the pond went on and on,
the hedgerows lacing greenfield after green,
and timeless ticking cows' tails upon
the garden's bounds affixed a boundless scene.
As upward stairs had swayed my pen to rise,
and nether lands had granted cool repose,

so I was Eye on all of earth and skies.
Can ruddy breaths and sounds these lengths disclose?
    Ah, children's cries, the sweetest music still,
    caught it all, this England, and the quill.

'The Rookery' New Buckenham, England, 1972

The sea often called to Chad. His 'Birds and Fishes', now that I
look back on it, forecast his experience with the heights and
depths of life.

Birds and Fishes

I set a ring of parched stones.
I gathered wood the shade of bones.
I hied me high o'er dimming tide
to lay this fire in eventide.
A day before this thought had burned
and setting store in dreams I yearned
to gather driftwood, kindle flame,
this dark and steaming seaside claim.

A lamp awaits the midnight sun
and shelter gives as shelter won.
The nips of light around the base
return my sight to quiet pace,
then larger twigs begin to boil.
From lamp-lit damp uncoil
the worms of passing summer's night.
Quietly I await the night

to nestle this unsettled land;
from birds to fishes it passes hand
where unworldly depths and sky meet
each day, plant and each retreat.
I haven't laughed like this again
or sung sweet heaven's songs, a din
to my very self. This eve I lay
on flats, the chilly lake at bay.

I'll give them back as all before
have wrested a moment, can wrest no more.
In a glance I recognize the call

to burn again the flotsam and all,
as once upon another shore,
the day my lyre was born and more,
this speckled star of mine began
and I to loving as I can.

The North Sea near Blakeney, Summer 1973

About this same time Chad began to contact his inner anima; this process was intimately connected with his writing of poetry. The following poem is based on a dream.

Meditations on Our Lady of the Fourth Rung

Tier Two

Mary walked through the room,
the proud and sauntering gait
as one destined to prize of art.
Tinkling was the chatter of
the articulate crowd;
confounding the elders was his Lady of Life.
Need Mary stop?
He urged her on to the stairs,
knowing no bow to appearance required.

A Meaningful Third

Together they climbed
the naked polished rungs
to another space
within, above,
Her station there
to await his release,
return,
nor was a blinking
to scar her eyes.

He Went On Alone

He sauntered in the chilly atmosphere
of still another chamber
yet above, yet further within,
the cavity
(we call ourselves Earth Mother).

Still, the silent morning had
not reigned light here,
chasm of wards and rooms,
asylum of the heart.
Neither death nor life
nor any spark burned,
modern dungeon aloft.
Care he would give,
care find,
for victims of psyche's blitz –
crowning conquest of deity –
Find, in the deepest of wilderness
our Lady of the Fourth Rung
whispering, fluttering night-soul,
clinging only to sagging breath,
closed eyelids
and slow circulation.

He had not the authority,
yet he unhooked the plastic bottle
of an unknown's blood,
fitted her channel to flow with his.
Friend of the fourth rung,
reviving, having begun
quietly, unclung
the lids of her dimness
to see him – missed and missed
in the tear-mist years,
knowing him alone
in whom her failures could be
sounded.

Slowly the life flowed
in the veins,
tasted its meal again,
squandered in a thousand cafés.
After the manner of teaching
he gave her to eat:
'This is my blood;
it shall be a new covenant
among you.'
It was with himself.

A longer poem flowed out of this period.

All Life a Unity

All life a unity,
said before, I'll say again,
and when by the moaning bar I put forth
and the twee weed lies reed between my teeth
and axemen lie in wait
then shall the fortress cease,
the waters part.

And I walked on dry ground.
And the tweedlebird was heard to sing,
loud and ringing,
by the stream . . .

The Old Stream

The stream of thought had wounded me,
the courage to be, and the more
I'd thought on it and colloquy
of seminars and far
reaches of reason and
marring of mental sparring –
the agile forgot in bull leaping afar
in Greece;
surcease had come in sleep.
I'd woke in afternoon
to find the door to death ajar
and the whiff of the eternal
caught in my nostrils,
a jingle going like this:
  why death at the end
  what was life then?
  'never before, never again . . .'

By the Stream

By the stream singing
sweet songs of my youth,
black spirituals bending
the nerves of heaven,
outburstings, cryings

solemn pleas
uttered in birthing, and birthings be.

In the meadows
I take my leave.
I walk among the daffodils,
am friend to the breeze.
Then I find the road,
small white stones broken.
The Roadmender was here,
entertaining children.
I stand by rushing waters
and hear the roar of forever.
These are my friends.
I shall roll them out on my mat
where the last ocean roll beckons
and I am heard no more.

I am. I've always been.
Whither I was before I do not know.
I have been in the election of the dead.
The sparks of my life were
    struggling centuries ago in
    Damascus, and in small prayer
    meetings in England, and later in
    the mountains of Virginia,
I encompass all my past, dim
    though my awareness be.
My sparks – my best convictions of
    what it is to be me –
    pray, tell will live on. Those
    who experience them be convinced,
    even as I have been, by others.

I've walked a never-never lane,
supped at a stream of might advent,
slept where paupers craved the rocks to
    cover them from inward wrath.
I've known the stream of consciousness,
wound the way of disbelief,
known every little crook of ruses,
    bent on ensnaring sparks of life.

I thought of his death.
I saw a thrush.
Life has ceased.
The skies opened:
bright light and tender shade,
mossy rock and water trilled
The Scottish mountain glade.
His Eleusinian field.
The sun gleams
through breaking clouds.
The bells ring
the nine o'clock of
eternity.

The next poem, late in Chad's stay in England, tells its own story.

The Winter of No Relenting

Like a winter of no relenting,
like a song in a flat key,
this wind blew stealthily, entering
the back door, unnerving me.
It was made of hate,
hate where no loathing
reached to an end and stopped
or met the foe imagined to be.
Only in the quiet pose
was it trimmed;
there where truth knocked
did I know he was unformed me.

It went deeper, this chilling wind,
deeper to where the promise
of tomorrow bayed,
deeper in the guts of marriage
where it would seem
neither could live with the other's path,
spiritual, except in that respect;
turned knife edge in the heart and found the dark.

Little Melton, England, 1977

It was a dark period in Chad's life. And there are no poems of real change until well after his return to North America. The mood begins to change with the following poem about dreams.

Dreams

Body image dreams are
of substance more powerful than celluloid,
more contrived than novels,
wedding times and remote places,
the wise owl of fortune, the seer,
the soul-image who is priceless.

I have knelt by dreams
and kissed dreams,
marched in the streets,
turning over the scenes
as a religious person handles a rosary
or enunciates a mantra.

Dreams have been my path,
like the glittering night beads
some child has re-found in the forest
and which lead the way back home;
beads, these turns of the mind
glimmering concrescences of all one is.

And lapping the
shore of eternity, like waves
in a moonlit night no one hears
or almost known, are dreams
or so they seem.

Then we wake up and handle them
like children born to us,
handle with affection and care,
not knowing fully whence they came,
knowing only they will grow up
and be our lives.

1981

This dream is interesting from the point of view of process work: 'Body image dreams are . . .' I heard Chad mention this image to Arnold Mindell when he first met Arnold, a couple of years after the poem's composition. It is, of course, similar to the dreambody as developed by Mindell. Mindell was thrilled to hear that Chad had had an inkling of the dreaming body, or dreambody, before the publication of his book *Dreambody: The Body's Role in Revealing the Self.* (Marie-Louise von Franz writes about this concept of synchronicity with respect to the appearance of ideas often in different parts of the world.)[1] Mindell has commented on the synchronicity of an idea appearing in many places when its time is right. Michael Fordham states in one of his essays that C. G. Jung conceived of the Self as being in the body.[2]

In the next chapter of Chad's life he had more to do with process work. He also continued to write poems. He tried to integrate the two interests, often writing poems after he had done powerful process work. The next two poems were born in this way.

Taj Mahal I

My teeth can relax.
I can meditate on Lao Tsu the Taoist,
can meditate in the midst of crowds,
watch passers-by melt from view,
engage not the fist
with the ready-to-fight foe.

No other watchword need I
but the light
travelling in the chin's muscles
and through the jaws,
those inevitable sinews
of deepening conflict
where the watch is the way
and the way is strife.

Never in my life
knew I this man settled
beneath those taut cheeks
where tons of tension congealed
whose man's name is Tao,

who lasts like the river,
nor is weary
of foes,
for they help him meditate.

He is meditating
on that golden tree,
crowning glint of the work
a bare flicker of the wind,
tingling branches of bone,
sea creatures, round, flat,
these petals
chiming like some Chinese knowing.

Taj Mahal II

Thine alabaster turrets glisten,
turning light into liquid,
running veins of purest stone
earth ever yielded of heart.

Never have I known words sharpened
so delicately to follow thy contours,
cresting layers of round loveliness,
following the form of the feminine.

Nor do the muted sounds raised
remain to speak in kind, immortal –
thy ribs have been, and rib cage,
which produced a sound all for all time.

That sound lingers here. In wonder
move it with your turbid finger.
You'll hear the air slice, a
vowel 'ove', vow love.

Immortal this man's devotion
to what he found through noble woman,
through self, through unlocking gates
and walking in the garden of powdered bliss.

You can meet him here still,
unlike the rest of us who left
that divine moment when

heart and body and form joined.
He asks no fare, our immortal.
Only raise your arms in awe
and know when you touch the fair
he, our laborer of bliss, is there.

There is really no end to Chad's story. Today he finds himself working with people in process groups. Occasionally he works with people who, like himself, have known great fear. Sometimes they have big processes and the fear of a lifetime changes. As a poet Chad picks up subtle signals as indications of the changing of one channel to another.

He told me about one such piece of work recently. A woman had been beset by fear for many years; on one occasion he noticed a switching in channels from auditory (internal dialog), which for her had been responsible for many years of weeping and stifled tears, to breaths. The small breaths, when amplified, became wind, powerful wind. And the emotions changed. Breath and breathing had given her a new lease on life. They were a powerful intervention, experienced at first as the smallest signal, in a situation in which she had been stuck: grief in the auditory channel. By finding her breath again her mind was calmed. Fear no longer controlled her experience.

Chad recounted this to me with a lot of excitement, and then he shared a poem he had written about a dream about two of our favorite characters from our New York days together in the 1960s, William Kennedy and Esther Harding, two of the founders of Jung's work in North America.

The Dream That Won't End

I sailed mid ports of life's last recalls.
I sailed with friends our greatest oceans' ends.
The hour of setting sun which none forestalls,
this hour the most cherished for love of friends:
we met again! In life as well our boon
to meet in hallowed room of peasants' inn
with spoons aside for closeness, unspaced like noon,
the holy gathering of kin exceeding kin.

Beyond Jung would trace the plan entire.
The snake consumed its end: Tibet arose;
I saw the summits lift, unveil their fire;
he glowed in lotus pose amidst the snows.
    The dream had chosen these souls in life relief
    to paint a continuum beyond belief.

Chad's inner work revealed that the imagination or the 'creative' is another formulation for process or the Tao. With some the creative may become directly the images of poetry or other arts. The record of their experiences in poems gives people the chance to go back at any time and connect again with deep moments when the current of life was experienced and was transformative.

9 • *Antoine: the Spirit in the Body*

I have some difficulty when writing about religious visions because some people, especially people working with the chronically mentally ill, might call Antoine crazy. He is a friend of mine who makes his living with his hands. I want to protect him from ridicule. I remember a not uncommon prejudice among psychiatrists that C. G. Jung was crazy.

Zorba is right. The only way to handle the confusion that dogs the reputation of both creative and spiritual people is to take on the criticism. In process work we have a way of doing this. It is founded on a view of the opposites. C. A. Meier has pointed out that a view of the opposites characterized many of the major Greek philosophers of the fifth to the third centuries BC. He adds that illness was imbalance in the opposites, whereas the way to health lay in balancing opposing energies.[1]

Process work takes this dynamism seriously, discovering that when we identify with either polarity, the other is also present. A rigid identity with sanity, for example, predicates the presence of insanity. Its presence is expressed by the denial of qualities which, in the hands of unbalanced people, may become extreme but of themselves are neutral. An example of such a quality is imagination.

Imagination is self-transcendence, the power to complete oneself from inside. Yet when people who work in institutions for the mentally ill see a client expressing imagination in an extreme way they attempt to write off the quality altogether. I say 'attempt to' because opposites cannot be destroyed: they merely take up residence in another part of the Self. Then, for example, imagination may express itself unconsciously in judging the motives of others through cross-projection.

Imagination is never lost. It is the light in the tunnel. I take up my imagination wholeheartedly. It is the psyche at play at

112

the point where a person stops growing. It flickers as awareness when, at the edge of one channel of information, such as the visual, one spontaneously shifts to another channel of information, let's say proprioception. To express imagination means continuously to be alive to the ever-shifting patterns present in the transactions between oneself and other people.

What makes the crazy person different from other people in expressing imagination? The fantasies of those in psychotic states lack the quality of transcendence, the capacity to see themselves as fantasizing, what Arnold Mindell calls a 'metacommunicator'. This communication function coordinates input about what is happening to one from all the channels of information – visual, auditory, proprioceptive, kinesthetic, etc. It is awareness *per se*.

Our secondary processes await us as fantasies. They await our process into awareness. What comes at first as a signal that our process is shifting to another channel of information – perhaps an unoccupied one – may become a doorway to our deepest selves, so that they may come into the world and inhabit it. For me that is intimately tied up with the mythological and religious figures that make up our own Western tradition. These figures, such as the Virgin, have lost their power for many people today.

C. G. Jung was a pioneer in this field. The implication of his work is that the mysteries of the Judeo-Hellenic-Christian tradition are realities of the inner world awaiting to be experienced individually by people. Esoteric traditions such as alchemy were a way of balancing what had become unbalanced in formal religious practice, bringing in the rejected darkness as well as the light. These lesser-known paths of the inner world also describe basic psychological processes of transformation.

In Jung's personal vision he saw himself as having been incarnated to carry further a philosophical development that had been at the heart of discussion in former times, namely the problem of the three and the four. He speaks of 'the development over the centuries of the divine triad and its completion with the feminine principle'.[2] He took immense satisfaction in the doctrine of the assumption of the Virgin into the triune god-head, which had formerly been considered masculine and was therefore incomplete. We find this shift towards placing a greater value on the feminine in the growing body of Jungian literature about the place of goddesses in human life.

Central to the theme of this chapter is an image that appeared in Antoine's dreams: that of lighting a candle. He called it the 'incandescent light'. It is the light of consciousness, which for me brings some understanding of certain of the principal figures of our Western tradition. It has a collective dimension. When people lose their connection with the deeper psychological forces, 'things fall apart', as W. B. Yeats has expressed it in 'The Second Coming'.

By contrast, when one person works on processing pain and anguish consciousness may become another experience altogether, such as the sense of a figure, larger than life, behind that person's life, giving meaning to it. If other people are present during process work, energies are released in them all. There is, for those present, no longer despair about the world. What works within process experiences in individuals, couples and small groups can also work in very large groups.

The incandescent light: we need a tale to represent the realities of the individuation process. A story retains the quality of being and non-being, 'form and emptiness', as the Heart Sutra says. This tale is about my friend Antoine. Not just another case history, it portrays how one person worked with spiritual, meditative processes.

In approaching the material it is important to realize that the psyche is fluid by nature. At its disposal is a range of images to represent certain structures of itself. The account that follows happens to concern the primary figures of the Christian tradition, the aspects of the god-head, which in the language of Jungian psychology we refer to as the god-image. (This leaves unanswered the question of what that image may be beyond psyche, but for our discussion that limitation is appropriate.) This understanding implies that images such as Christ may be very similar to Buddha in their essence. One may dream of the powerful image of the Self in figures from other religions and folk traditions. Indeed, I know Antoine has encountered in his dreams the god-image in other guises.

There is some value in using material from any one of the

Judaic, Hellenic or Christian traditions. It is familiar to many people in the West, though for many today specific religious images have faded, with immense loss. When the image of the Self has been repressed people may sense that the more profound meaning of their lives has diminished. But the Self is not found in religion alone; it contains all the opposites as well. This may become clearer as Antoine's dreams and visions unfold.

A point of historical comparison comes specifically from Hellenistic times. During the first few centuries of this aeon, prior to Constantine, visitations by the gods in dreams were a major feature of life. This was true of the whole area of the Hellenistic world from northern England to Syria, from Spain to as far as the Black Sea, as Robin Lane Fox points out. People erected statuary and shrines to commemorate the visitation of a god or goddess in a dream. Art, poets, including Homer, polytheism and a prevalent attitude toward the gods that established them as friends and helpers – all these were the expressions of a world view in which goddesses and gods kept company with people from different social strata.[3] This world was also imbued with a philosophy that acknowledged the saving and healing powers of the goddesses and gods. To the Greeks the gods were forces beyond human control, personifications of forces in the universe. They often assumed the role of protectors. During this period no orthodoxy or institution prescribed what one could believe or experience; people were not nervous about heresy.

The disappearance of heterodoxy in the West brought with it a problem: belief dominated experience, and people began to test experience on the basis of belief rather than the reverse. In time the yardstick of experience was discarded altogether in favor of faith.

The loss of heterodoxy also undermined orthodox views. When other opinions, or information from the secondary process, are not honored even what one identifies with may itself become slightly distorted. We see this in the tendency to literalize religious terms and practices, which may be the consequence of a desire to protect them from all other influences. Any attempt to construct a perfect model of dogma in which all believe subverts the truth of the model, making it exclusive, defensive, rather than flexible and tolerant. Religious truths may then become, in the minds of some, unchanging, fixed and literal, rather than capable of encompassing what happens in real life and what is, by nature, symbolic and inner.

Jung had a wonderful phrase: 'symbolic therefore real'. What is experienced at the level of the inner life of individual men and women has an unmistakable ring of truth about it, especially if it is also found, in similar form, in the experiences of those who specifically develop the inner life – contemplatives, saints, poets, people on the path of individuation – and particularly if comparisons can be found in other cultures and religious traditions and in other times. Such, indeed, is the experience of the student of comparative mythology.

To give but one example: Joseph Campbell points out that there are two outlooks on reality that make their appearance in many of the different cultures of the world and in various epochs: an experience of spirit protectors and a sense of something that extends beyond this lifetime.[4] This is heterodoxy at its best. To those who identify with orthodoxy, an acknowledgment of such universal beliefs could be of value, since it might nurture a less literal attitude and give more berth to the Spirit.

Antoine told me about his background. As a young child he was fascinated with the beauty of the female and drawn irresistibly to it. He would spend days at his grandmother's house in order to ride his bicycle in the mornings to where he hoped to catch a glimpse of the girl he loved, another elementary-school-age child who didn't even know he cared. He and I agreed that this had been one of the beginnings of his interest in his soul.

He was very much involved in dating girls during his adolescence, yet his mystical side developed as well, and he would have a secret communion with his soul as he enjoyed nature on early-morning walks at summer camp. There were other times in his adult life when the beauty of someone else would communicate itself to him. He said that this sense connected him with all the persons with whom he had been close.

Antoine told me he dreamed once of beauty embodied in the mistress of El Greco. He mused about El Greco teaching her love

and her teaching him courage during the time of the Inquisition
in Toledo. Antoine felt it was that courage which releases
people's creativity, their inner experience of life and its mysteries,
in a world that seems hostile to such manifestations of the
feminine.

He had a series of dreams that he wanted to tell me about.
The first concerned a Jewish woman, pictured in a famous
photograph, evincing bravery at the head of a column of her
people being led by Nazi soldiers down a European street. About
this dream he wrote the following:

> I am thinking
> throughout my life
> I must succour
> the Jewish woman
> driven from her home.
> I languish in the
> sufferings of the Italian
> Jews separated from their homes.
> I am angered by anyone who
> blames them for being overpowered.
> I, too, have been overpowered
> by an analyst in my youth.
>
> Once before I fell in love
> in a spell with an anima
> figure who looked like the
> woman driven from her home
> by the Nazis
> in the famous photograph.
> How terrible, how Hitlerish.
> She is leading the pack
> of persons arrested from
> their normal lives, removed
> from all human comforts
> by a blind, bizarre power.
> She is most beautiful,
> most cultured, most European.
> This one who has suffered so,
> she is my anima soul;
> I always know she is the one

most like me.
I can never be quiet
in a Christian church –
she is not there.

She is one of the body,
she is one of light and
    dark of the Psalms,
she is one knowing both
    sides of YAHWEH,
she oriented to humor
    in the face of life
with wry laughs and jokes
    at all anomalies,
even of her people,
even of defeat
at times almost
of the greatest mysteries,
and she I must remember
is also Hasidic,
taking joy
as rebound of anguish,
a side I don't know
in my own Jewish soul.

For a quarter of a century
it is she who carries
my inner feeling,
so much so
I dreamt of being
in the synagogue –
a dream incomplete
because I would not glimpse
the play on women's bodies
being shown,
thinking this beneath
my psychological duty
to develop my relation
to my anima;
I could not start there,
peer then
into what seemed

purely the mysteries of the body –
Christian split!

And, yes, I offered
this synagogue dream
to my teacher, a token
to identify with him totally,
to be in his religion with him,
but all my attempts
were misplaced;
I never told him I loved him so
I wanted to be with him
in his religion too,
maybe something not so easy
for all the centuries
of persecuting Christians,
not so easy.

Then in my recent dream
I thought my dear anima
in the guise of the woman,
the one fleeing in the picture,
and yet not her –
I thought these were the seeking
presence of all my yearnings:
not so,
beneath all yearnings
He appeared,
Christ with his lantern
in the deep darkness,
his imploring look,
his integrated crown of thorns,
his eyes of wisdom and compassion
    for humanity.

The soul I thought was suffering
had led instead
to the Self,
the complete Human
the many-petaled,
rounded experience
image of God in the person,
mankind delivered from its suffering

> much as the step
> of Buddha
> in his four noble truths,
> when suffering is no longer master
> but a divine image
> shrouded in part and in inner light.

Norwich, in East Anglia, England, was a place where Antoine went in his dreams, a place of sublime beauty. He said he would often dream of a chapel there built into the hillside: in his dream life he would find it over and over again. It was down a narrow, very old street, which was at times an arcade, and on the street he passed an old ward of a nineteenth-century hospital. In the hidden, inner church was true mystical experience, unencumbered by modern thinking processes forbidding this or disproving that. Here he was simply himself, surrounded by the mysteries. Part of the place of worship trailed off into the earth itself, where there were old bones from previous centuries. There he was at home. It was the place, with its unceasing candlelight, of his immortal soul.

Norwich is a place of mind. There are the marks of history, sites where people were cared for in hospitals, perhaps as a result of the efforts of Elizabeth Fry and Edith Cavell. There may also be felt the beginning immobilization of the human spirit as the new industry of towns uprooted people from the countryside, family, the archetypal realities of religion. Beyond the hospital there is the chapel. Perhaps its candles will flourish in all times, hidden partly beneath the earth's surface, merging into ancient soil. There, if there were spirit protectors, they would pray for the world. Antoine said, 'Here in this place my soul findeth rest, both now and in eternity.'

He continued with the dream. The woman in it was no longer an unidentified anima figure but the Virgin Mary. He saw her dressed in a long, full skirt, somewhat like that depicted in Grünewald's painting. He was several feet away, and he sensed a union with her. Then followed a vision of the Holy Spirit as a bird with its beak pointed down over the Virgin's head, the prelude of Christ's incarnation.

In my view, Antoine's dreams and experiences had begun to parallel closely those of the alchemists. Fortunately, I had just finished reading Jung's description of the alchemist's concept of the third stage of the alchemical process. The first stage was separation from one's emotions (in the sense of no longer being identified with them). The second stage was union, not just the union of a male and female but called, among other things, the 'chemical marriage'; one image for it is that of a dragon uniting with a woman in her grave. Jung had this to say about the third stage: 'a consummation of the *mysterium coniunctionis* can be expected only when the unity of the spirit, soul and body is made with the original *unus mundus*. This third stage of the *coniunctio* was depicted after the manner of an Assumption and Coronation of Mary, in which the Mother of God represents the body.'[5]

As it happened, Antoine told me about lying in his bed in the morning and experiencing consciously what he was experiencing in his body (proprioception). He pointed out that some people might be threatened by Western attitudes, which promoted constant activity and prohibited the touching of one's own body. His experience had been quite different. He said that first of all he experienced pain when he probed deep with his finger just above his navel. The pain seemed to move to other places; he would simply follow it. Sometimes when he felt his feet or calves he experienced contentment beyond words.

Antoine's exploration of the proprioceptive channel is similar to what Arnold Mindell describes as 'process meditation'[6] (to be explained fully later in this chapter). When one's thoughts are not constricted, it is hard to say what may arise. This is especially true of feelings – and not only emotions but physical sensations, even sexual ones, as well. Process work is a veritable window opening on to what really matters in humankind, the soul and, through it, eternity.

Antoine was willing to follow my encouragement and to write down his dreams. He noticed that it was the first time since his youth that he had allowed himself to spell God with a capital 'G'. He dreamed that God was a man and that man was a god. Man expressed himself by wearing a bright red shirt and moving in an outward direction towards God. And then, as the red-shirted man returned like a finger entering his chest, it was as if God were entering the human domain. It was a divine mystery, Antoine said.

Antoine switched channels from visual to proprioceptive as he began to be aware of his breathing. A meditation formed around White Tara, a Tibetan Buddhist deity. Antoine, the meditator, sent out blessings to the gathered deities and received their blessings in return. He said the breathing helped him, and occasionally he would break into a song (switching channels from proprioceptive to auditory).

I told him that there is something about a human being that is god-like. Jung thought of it as the capacity to make the world emerge into full existence by being conscious of it, and therefore by being a part of the world that has become conscious of itself. On the other hand, God is man-like or woman-like, revealing wisdom and compassion and expressing in one person both the elements and the cosmos.

During the weeks when these dreams were incubating inside Antoine, he said he felt a tremendous burden because to experience visions of the god-head, male and female, and to have these come to him as they did, in an unconventional form, seemed to make him special. Two things happened almost immediately that brought him relief: first, he discovered, through a chance conversation over breakfast with a Buddhist friend, that such experiences were a regular part of esoteric practice in Tantric Buddhism. Secondly, in church that same day he discovered several other things that seemed relevant to his soul-searching and also synchronistic. It was the second Sunday of the new year and the celebration of Christ's baptism. During the service the priest said the same words that Antoine had heard with some amazement in his waking dream of the morning: 'This is my beloved Son in whom I am well pleased.' Then he recalled that all Christians are meant to experience the Christ-nature of their own deeper Selves.

There was nothing special about him in this respect. What was special was his having been born human and the capacity of all human beings to realize their connection with the god-head,

to know that Jesus, Mary, the Holy Spirit and God are powerful
parts of the Self and alive in themselves. It was a tremendous
relief to Antoine to realize that he was part of a community, both
present and historical, in which others had such experiences.
And he felt that the capacity to bring such experiences to the
community, to share in others' visions, was a further realization
of his role as part of the mystical body of Christ.

What I want to say to members of all faiths is that the
mysteries of the great religious traditions are part of the potential
of the individual soul. It is as if the mysteries are waiting to be
worked out in all our lives. I hope for this realization in us all.
From Antoine's and others' experiences I realize now that
mystical visions may take place when people allow themselves a
full range of fantasy. But it does not mean, in most cases,
literalizing fantasy, thinking that it has to do with actual persons
and actions. Fantasy is a dream of the soul, the inner life.

With his dream of the god-head, of God, Antoine felt that
something was completed in himself. As Jung has said, the
individuation process follows the pattern of shadow, anima and
then Self. For Antoine the god-image was the image of Self in its
completeness. All the projections, all the fights with others and
inner anguish, all the smiles, flirtations and glimpses of insight
were intended for this moment when the inner part of him took
form: the god-image in the human being, the completeness that
is the original condition of the human being.

Antoine's story, as I have suggested, parallels the stages of
alchemy. When he was young he had many struggles with others.
At first he could not separate himself from his emotions. Then
gradually he was able to be the witness of his fear, so to speak.
He experienced separation from his emotions, the *separatio*, as the
alchemists called it. In the next phase of his life he had at first
been taken with women, falling in love with them in his heart.
This stage too had involved many struggles. The flesh was
tempted, and instinct seemed to have little time for anything but
itself. But he had kept faith with his desire to be true to himself.
He told me he had always known that there was something
behind desire for a woman: it was the woman in him. Now and
again he had an experience of what Jung called anima or soul.

Those experiences, he recounted with a sigh and wide eyes, were sublime. They were like what the alchemists called the second stage, the chemical marriage. But there was still more: the *mysterium coniunctionis* of the third stage. Antoine described it thus. He could acknowledge that there was no difference between high and low, farthest and nearest – all were contained in some kind of unity with each other. This helped him to understand how at one point his spiritual perception could be dominated by an image of the sublime divine and at the next a golden receptacle; by the Virgin Mary and earth; by the phallus and the light of the Light of the World; by women's bodies and erections and the Holy Spirit blowing where it will. The *mysterium coniunctionis* was all things accepted on their own terms, where the simplest could also be the most subtle, where all images seemed to be those of creative life energy itself. Then he quoted Mother Theresa, who spoke of meeting Christ 'in the life lived'. He was ready to do that now.

In my last session with Antoine he told me that he hoped his visions about the triune god being completed with the feminine to become a quaternity would inspire others. He said that for him happiness came from being inspired, from loving people without any reluctance, all his warmth going out to them. He laughed and said, 'To think, all this began with an early dream of meeting the Christ figure and fleeing from the possibility of wholeness, the image of the realized Self.' He no longer wondered about his place or worried about anything particular, he said. Just that day, when he was in church, he had realized that when he was a young man he could have enjoyed being a priest and seeing others take pleasure in his manifestation of spirit, admiring him and focusing their attention on him. Now, catching a glimpse of himself out of the limelight, so to speak, he was free to give. Nothing stood in the way of his manifesting the Self in himself. He said that the rest of his vision took place in his favorite Greek restaurant. There he knew the happy music, the energy of the Mediterranean world – that ancient world where the opposites of spirit and body, masculine and feminine, are united in one joy that is beyond words.

Antoine's experience of the four aspects of the Christian god-head is an experience of the spirit that resides in psyche/body unity, found in the body as image, feeling and movement. The experiences of people like Antoine indicate that the deep values that have resided in our religious traditions, together with their more esoteric counterparts (such as alchemy), are still very much alive in the inner realm.

The alchemical tradition has sometimes been regarded as the dark side of Christianity. Barbara Hannah mentions a comment of Jung's about Christianity having identified itself almost solely with the light side, rejecting the more chthonic darkness. Jung said that the world into which Christ had been born was so dark that His identification with the light was necessary in order to preserve it.[7] In the cause of wholeness, however, these elements later needed to be added again, in the individual soul at least. Alchemy is a collective manifestation of the process of restoring to the human image these qualities: matter, nature, the feminine, non-virtue and earth.

What was alive in Antoine's dreamlife was the Self. Father, Son and Holy Spirit, together with the Virgin Mary, are but one representation of wholeness, the Self. Wholeness in which the Self is experienced and represented has the greatest value. It is 'worshipped'. It is the incorruptible substance, the lapis, gold as an inner reality, the immortal part of the soul.

There are ways to find this wholeness, to experience aspects of the Self. The Self, by definition, contains opposites. Therefore our natural fear about the possible imbalance of religion or spirit is met with the knowledge that in wholeness of psyche/body, religion and spirit are balanced by their opposites and those opposites, in turn, are balanced by religion and spirit.

Dreams and visions gave Antoine the capacity to live out of his deeper Self. Some people – productive, decent people by collective standards – lack the motivation to realize in their lifetime something of the deeper Self. Yet it is the Self that motivates one to live fully, to exploit all one's capacities, to open others to those capacities in themselves.

Often the motive force behind this lifetime is a spirit figure like the one that my friend Aristotle first experienced in a dream and later sought in Greece. Such a figure may motivate one to do various things, perhaps to do all one can to help others find the deeper Self behind their own sufferings and ailments, personal and interpersonal. Whatever the Self may motivate one to do, it seems sooner or later to come up against the suffering of the world and to want to make a creative attempt to transmute that suffering at some level of the collective. It means to take on all the parts of one's life: one's family and the family of the world; one's health and the health of those one meets; one's own resources and the resources released when others come in touch with their deeper Self. These ideas are but examples; what one does, and wants to do, depends on the particular figure discovered in the recesses of the human psyche/body.

Spiritual processes are not for everyone. For some people the spiritual path may be their primary process, the one they identify with; in their case there is the possibility that further consciousness will come through it. To others spiritual processes may be those with which they do not identify; in their case the possibility of spiritual or mystical experiences may reside in the more powerful secondary processes. To this group the story of Antoine and the procedures outlined in this chapter may be a resource for further exploration.

In process work no one should be spiritual or not-spiritual. The important thing is to follow one's processes wherever they lead. Often it is the secondary process that has the healing effects.

I was once invited to a Midwestern state of the United States to give a workshop. Before going I had the impression that life there was probably hard for some as a result of the large, collective industrial processes in which they were involved. What I discovered astonished me. Several people in the workshop had had extraordinary mystical experiences that had emerged from the proprioceptive and kinesthetic channels of information, which were not the customary areas used by them. Such experiences I refer to as mystical because they involve certain themes and figures that have been prominent in several world religions. They also have an intensely practical effect because they offer information that guides people to the processes underlying their suffering and difficulties and casts the problem in an entirely new light. The problem can then be approached from a different angle. People generally work on their problems in their occupied channels, and there they go round and round. The less accessible, unoccupied channels often contain the large experiences that are transformative.

Sometimes I begin a workshop with process meditation as described by Arnold Mindell in a chapter entitled 'Working Alone on Yourself' in his *Working with the Dreaming Body*. I will outline that procedure here briefly.

Process meditation begins with a person asking him or herself: what channel of information am I in? For example, someone in a problem-solving mode might be in the auditory channel of information; she or he might be engaged in an inner dialog, voicing the various parts of the argument, directions or admonitions. Or the channel might be sensory, focusing on pain.

Having answered this first question, the person is ready to move on to the second step, which is to amplify what is going on in the channel of information concerned. The pitch of the internal dialog is raised and the talk is allowed to get speedier and more intense, for example, or, if one is working with a pain in the stomach, that pain is intensified. Once amplification has been applied, it won't be long before the person shifts to another mode or channel; this is done more or less involuntarily. Then he or she is working in another channel of information.

As a third step this secondary channel, and its contents, are amplified. Several more channel switches may occur. Eventually, something new will happen, a surprise that will indicate that the person is truly on another pathway. He or she should stick with that surprising material, following it with detailed attention. That will be the new point of awareness that can help to reorganize the way in which the person is approaching life. In the depths of the personality too something will have been touched – perhaps the life energies have been rearranged in a new pattern.

How could I use this meditation? you may ask. First of all, determine whether you tend to get lost and confused in your own reactions. If so, seek out someone with experience and an appreciation of you that will enable you to undertake this exercise. You may want to tell your partner that the process approach does not move you away from the painful and the threatening; rather, it pushes you through it as long as supports are there. (Perhaps you will want to work with a qualified process worker in one of the many workshops available in many countries.)

One way in which to bring relationship and spiritual processes together is to arrange to spend some time with a close friend who has become acquainted with process procedures. Tell your friend that you would like to tell him or her about some of your mystical experiences, dreams or visions. After you have begun your description, you may become aware that you are moving in your chair, or scratching, or that an unusual tone has come into your voice, or that you are staring at something. If you realize that you are giving a signal from a different channel, follow it and describe to your friend what happens. The signals that we do not intend to give are double signals. They can be processed along the same lines as described earlier.

Religious visions may be the equivalent of body experiences (body in the sense of dreambody). Processing such visions with a relationship partner is very likely to extract more of their meaning. However, *pan metron ariston* ('all that which is balanced is excellent'), the Greeks thought. Religious visions are fine; they belong to one part of the personality. If one can also have love for people and, better still, an effective means of processing relationship feelings with them, then all the better.[8]

Many patients in mental hospitals have lost the confidence to work through relationship problems with others, a fact compounded by a loss of power on their part to have a real say in their own destinies. They have religious visions, but they often lack the comforting, guiding reality of a friend, someone with whom to dance their visions. Sometimes the capacity to witness the vision, the so-called metacommunicator of process work, is also absent. All the channels of communication are needed if one is going to have spiritual visions. Then Jesus, Buddha, Isaiah,

Lao Tsu and other spiritual leaders can come into one's life, one's *Living*.

At the beginning of this chapter I alluded to an image that came up in one of Antoine's dreams: the incandescent light. I had asked him if I could convey his dreams of quaternity here, if he could decide whether it was right to bring these sacred mysteries into the light of day, where people could read of them and ponder them. I told him that there might be negative reactions in cultures where some repudiate the mysteries in such forms. There was one dream that, for him, seemed like an answer to my question: I relay it here in Antoine's words.

The Flame

There was a big occasion. The Dalai Lama was speaking. I hung about the front wanting to be close to him when he spoke. Then some candles were going out. Some Boy Scouts were attending to them, but they couldn't keep them from going out. I had one match and from bringing it near a wick of a red candle a flame began to burn. Then I blew and blew on it and it became the pure, white light. The whole crowd was watching me. This was the Quaternity experience, the candles – the Christian experience as an experience of the inner life.

When people truly follow their own experience, it is possible that they may dream about something that may be of value not only to themselves but also to others. Antoine's dreams, and my experiences with people in the Midwestern United States, are indications to me that spiritual life is a powerful secondary process for many people. As long as such processes are not literalized but remain symbolic of the Self, their general effect – like following the Tao – can lead experiencers to more openness and to the greater personality that may lie beneath the surface.

The story of the spirit is in the dream; the story of the body is in the dream. The ancient Greeks believed firmly that dreams offered information about sickness and health. In dreams too we travel to faraway places during a single night. Our spirit walks among ancient rocks, up old hills and within shrines of former epochs. These places signal the deepest part of us, the Self, which one day will no longer exist as we know it today, and dreams may guide the days when we are in the body and walk among trees and flowers and the friends of this life, keeping us in touch with the greater Self.

Antoine was needed to complete these accounts. In process work I find that deep spiritual experiences lie behind 'problems', which are like states with which people may identify themselves.

Antoine's spiritual experiences belong here in another sense too. The deep pain of psychosis and of spiritual experiences is partly the product of their being associated in the collective mind with fear and misunderstanding. Therefore deep shame and secrecy are often the experience of both the psychotic and the spiritual. Psychosis and spirituality are both wounded conditions in need of redemption from personal rejection.

There is a further relationship between these states and process work. After working with people in analysis for some time, I have found that some of them describe earlier experiences of a visionary or synchronistic nature, though they associate such phenomena with the bizarre and even the psychotic. Often, as a result of this, a dark cloud hovers over their entire perception of themselves, related, perhaps, to a time of depression, fear or anxiety. The exploration of past experiences within the perspectives of larger emergent processes extending over a lifetime, or even beyond the present life, can be a turning point in our work together; such are the perspectives of the dream in the body. When the Self, the dynamism for wholeness, is discovered within such experiences they can be accepted. Often acceptance of earlier experiences is followed by powerful spiritual dreams, as if the wounds inflicted by visionary and synchronistic experiences were followed by the redemption of genuine spiritual experience and release into the creative.

Such is my hope for all who suffer.

10 • Conclusion

What is the connection between psychotic, spiritual and creative processes? As far as this study is concerned, the four architects are meant as a balance to the six psychiatric clients. If energy is lived outwardly, as in the case of the four architects, the possibilities for spiritual and creative development are enormous.

The architects have within the scope of their lives the capacity to develop to an extent suggested by Heraclitus' statement that the boundaries of consciousness are unknown. They are creative people, and, as we have seen, their interests in individuation and in spiritual development are highly developed. Their lives and energies can be immensely fruitful. Many psychiatric patients, by contrast, seem to grow downward as their energies are directed towards dark, cold regions of the mind.

Above or below ground, however, many patterns of energy are the same. To present four creative people beside the six more interior persons of the study is to raise the hope that those condemned to a twilight existence within the mental health system and outside it may yet be released through creative approaches, such as process work, to experience the clear light of mind. In the case of Chad, for example, a rich internal and spiritual world was transmuted into poetry, another option of inner development and of process work. Only as processes are worked with can they move beyond the stasis recognized by pathology. All conditions – chronic body problems, relationship problems, minor and severe psychological problems – can be worked with through process work in a way that releases the energy to move on.

Often psychiatric patients respond to only one channel of information. They try valiantly, but unsuccessfully, to work out every difficulty in the auditory channel, for example. In some ways their difficulties can be seen to begin with the restriction of channels of information. The creative person, by contrast, lives and works in all the channels of information, and there is a tremendous interplay between them as they switch back and forth. Process work, in general, is creative in its following of subtle switches in information channels. As many difficulties arise when people fail to relate to information provided by all the channels of information, process work provides an answer, in that it releases creativity. Chad's poetry is illustrative of this creative process of being; he became more alive to all the channels of information and was more expressive as a consequence.

My book ends, as it began, on a religious note. Jung defines religion etymologically: *religio* means to 'bind again'. In this work about the body, which is based upon Jungian psychology, I am linked with what has always been important to me: *the ineffable in life*. We think that we should find that in a place of worship, but we don't always find it there. We may find the ineffable in body experience when the Self, which is contained there, has been neglected for many years. Mindell writes about this in *Dreambody*:

> the worst demons are insensitive attitudes toward the body. When people finally feel their body center, they experience extreme loneliness and sadness because the body center, the Self, has been neglected in the rush and pressure of everyday life. As soon as they reach this center, they often break down, racked with sobs, crying out of their sadness. At least temporarily this may dissolve the divisive rigidity characteristic of consciousness.[1]

This leads us to the subject of the soul, or anima, and the dreambody.

The Soul and Dreambody

For this work to be complete I must take you on an excursion. Searching for a name in a seminary library, I came upon many volumes of the journal *Spring*. *Spring* today is an account of soul, though it dates back to a time when it was the voice of the Jung Club in New York, an organization in which one of my mentors,

Conclusion

M. Esther Harding, a psychiatrist, was a very strong influence. Her work was to show how the element that we associate with religion, namely wonder at the synchronistic, is present in inner experiences. One does not have to study Jung's life very deeply to realize that the same was true of his life. Fordham tells how a scroll replica of the Shroud of Turin hung behind an inner and private door in Jung's study. Why all these associations with religion? Let's let the soul offer its answer as a form of introduction to dreambody work.

Jungian psychology
has become very thinking-oriented
and moved away from the subtle processes.

I call upon Jungians and others
to imagine within the body again.

What we have to say
should describe those high points
in our lives when
we knew ourselves
for who we really are –
there was no question then
we felt something in our bodies.
I doubt that the experiences were really separated.

Journey then with me
into the material of process-oriented psychology.
I couldn't be just thinking for you.
The material won't allow it.
I begin with the
imaginal,
a new vision of psychology.[2]
Now I lead into the body.
Will you come?
My left hand goes up.
I touch finger to thumb
and open up.

Even though I am prepared to talk, I do not begin.
You ask first the silver-tongued
the man acquainted with images

the imaginal
poesis
(In me) that relates to my little introduction to the book,
relates to a part of me, which is poetic and somewhat
    scholarly,
talking about the body and process from this
perspective.

Process is not easy to put into words.
Process describes when things happen spontaneously
    of their own accord,
        as if they are moved from some internal
        image or source.
You can see a process.
An image is acting out;
Soul is becoming flesh.
That is process.

Let me describe to you 'process'.
If I have words
and if I have pen,
well, is that process then?
Process is a doc
mulling over the behavior of a patient,
like the physician in
The French Lieutenant's Woman
who is thinking about this person
and realizing something crucial
is about to happen to her,
worthy of his meditation, his thoughts
that the now is present
and demanding.
And he can't think of moving
out of it to tie his shoes
or empty his wastebasket
because
something lies deep there in the realization,
something like Von Hartmann[3]
has written.
He must put it all together.
It is coming together in him:
that client,

134

her crisis,
his reading,
himself –
that is process!

Process is not wanting to intellectualize
or even think.
Process sees.
Body speaks to body;
a lip curls;
a shoulder lifts;
the eyes get red.
He is choosing to speak:
he would rather tell you this
than what he is saying with words.
'He' is inner.

He wants to contradict the word-maker 'I'.
He has something more vital to say.
He has been waiting a century to speak.
He is in the man.
'She' is in the woman.
BODY
SOMA – PERSONALITY:
in the muscles, in feeling,
in suggestion, vagueness, yearning,
not quite understood feelings.
GESTURES
are this inner source's voice.
No one listens.

I am sorry for you, dear soul.
You were told
early on
you only *reside* in the body.
You can leave on death,
not contaminated by flesh.
Oh, the pain you have felt!
For centuries you've been persecuted.
You reside in the whisper,
the deep, dark sigh
which lasts over the brink of despair.

Poesis,
poesis gives you room
to breathe in.
Wordsworth walking down a road
in
brief moments
when the imagination is free.

(My audience):
'I thought you said
the body –
the imagination and
the body are different.'
'The imagination can fly.
Just try that with the body.'
I don't mean
just what souls mean.
I am a soul,
but I'm in the body too.
You see that's the meaning of anima.
Anima is not just the soul –
she is body.

She can be troubled.
Watch her wander:
the fingers start to be
        rubbed by the thumbs.

There is no difference,
my brothers and sisters.

The self can't
have its territory
staked out,
so that body
lies outside
imaginal, soul.
She is lovely there
in all her radiance.

How could I have
missed our meeting?
When my body starts to perspire
and I don't bother her,

when I am very tense
and I go ahead and eat,
when I drive myself,
making those sacrifices of rest and solace,
she suffers.

She is not just
in some woman's
soft and well-cared-for skin.
She is me, CORPUS.

When I lie down to sleep at night
she is present.
When I do Tai Chi, she lives.

Sometimes I do deep body work –
then I find out
what she is about;
she is my soul.
When I find her
there is no more searching;

as an ancient prayer said,
'nearer than hands and feet'.

Anima or Soul is Body

About the anima. Emma Jung speaks of three anima figures from
Scandinavian mythology, Wurd, Wendandi and Skuld, as
appearing 'to embody the natural life process of becoming and
passing away'.[4] I like that verb 'embody'. I think it is meant in
more than just a metaphorical sense. The anima embodies the
unconscious. The body is (part of the) unconscious. Sudden
flushes in men not acquainted with their feelings, tingling – these
are examples of the link between the body and the unconscious.
When these somatic processes are going on at the same time, you
know you have contacted an area of commonality – feeling in
relationship and feeling in the body.

The title of Emma Jung's essay is 'The Anima as an Elemental
Being'. She writes: 'The concept of elemental beings dwelling in
water and air, in earth and fire, in animals and plants, is age-old

and occurs all over the world, as is shown by countless examples in mythology and fairy tales, folklore, and poetry.'[5] She comments on how similar these patterns are to dreams of modern people.

Mindell's book *Dreambody* explores how such elemental beings, elements and processes may represent processes in the body. He writes: 'The plants in our tale are vegetative nourishment. "Vegetative" implies involuntary action and life in the body. Involuntary activities include the peristaltic motions of the viscera and heart, pupil dilation and general states induced by meditation, dreams, and drugs.'[6]

In dreams or body experiences the anima will appear spontaneously as the water nixie or sprite, the nymph. This is the form that the anima assumes in fairy tales, according to Emma Jung. And that same elemental being (easily translated as body) is as Jung points out 'the initial stage of the individuation process'. In her other, more divine, aspect the anima is Sophia, wisdom.

The experiences I have reported in Chapters 3–6 are unusual for people in institutions. I cannot explain fully why the dreambody therapy should have had such an effect, although one explanation may be this: each person's own processes constituted the therapy itself. There is a certain awe attendant as one experiences dreambody. The connection between deep dreambody experiences and something like religious experience can be seen in Mindell's statement: 'All the figures of the psychic pantheon – the gods, snakes, the anima, animus and self – have physiological counterparts ... The physiological corollary of the Self, the organizing power behind psycho-physical processes, is the dreambody.'[7]

The Self is Jung's choice of word for the self-organizing principle, the subject of devotion of many religions. We also learn about the dreambody in its alchemical sense through Tibetan Buddhist meditation. Hugh Downs writes: '*Mani* means jewel; to Sherpas this word recalls the invocation, or mantra, "*Om Mani Padme Hum*". This epithet of the deity of compassion, Avalokitesvara, means "He who holds the jewel and lotus". *Mani* represents the treasures and wealth associated with lucid vision; it corresponds to the philosopher's stone of the Europeans.'[8]

All of the four exploring clients gleaned important information from the non-verbal, proprioceptive channel. Joy located her caring feelings in her heart, and she made a start in exploring the position, and change of position, of her bent and moving foot through resistance, which took her into the experience of floating. Rose's first experience of her spirit, in times of deep trouble, arose from the proprioceptive experience of being covered and having pressure exerted on her enfolded limbs and torso. Monie's first experience of psychological awareness, of 'yucko', the intolerable thought and image, came when my co-therapist put the burden of her weight on Monie's back. The decisive experience in Albert's world was the discovery of pain in his knees; with it came the first experience, in recent years, of himself, of his feeling (anima) – an opportunity to relate to himself.

The four architects undertook another kind of excursion. In their case a process born in dreams was waiting to be lived out in the world channel and in relationships. Strange spiritual dreams are also a process waiting to be discovered by those of us who have precious human life. The lives of my friends and analysands Chad and Antoine teach me that human life is a process that leads to the fully awakened, whole being. Their lives seem to be developing in the direction of the recognition and realization of the meaning of their existence.

What is the spirit figure behind your life? If you don't know, I hope you will explore it as intently as did my friend Aristotle, so you too may discover why you are here.

Notes and References

2 Dreambody Work: the Foundation, the Method and the Clients

1. Neil Michlem, 'On Hysteria: the Mythical Syndrome', *Spring*, 1974, p. 155.
2. T. G. Pautler, MD, 'Parkinson's Disease, Immobility and the Repression of Psychosis' (mimeo.), 1985.
3. Neil Michlem, 'The Intolerable Image: the Mythic Background of Psychosis', *Spring*, 1979, p. 16.
4. Michael Fordham, 'Jungian Views of the Body–Mind Relationship', *Spring*, 1974, pp. 166–78.
5. Arnold Mindell, *City Shadows: Psychological Interventions in Psychiatry*, London and New York, Routledge & Kegan Paul, 1988.
6. He was there serving Vietnamese children under the auspices of the American Friends Service Committee.
7. Martin Buber, *I and Thou*, New York, Charles Scribner's Sons, second edition, 1958.
8. Arnold Mindell, *The Dreambody in Relationships*, London and Boston, Routledge & Kegan Paul, 1987.

4 Rose

1. C. G. Jung, *Psychology and Alchemy, Collected Works*, Vol. 13, pp. 269–71.
2. M. Esther Harding, *Psychic Energy: Its Source and Its Transformation*, Washington, DC, The Bollingen Foundation, second edition, 1963, p. 174.

5 Monie

1. Neil Michlem, 'The Intolerable Image: the Mythic Background of Psychosis', *Spring*, 1979, p. 16.
2. Tarthang Tulku, *Skillful Means*, Berkeley, Dharma Publishing, 1978, p. 3.

6 Albert

1. Marie-Louise von Franz, *Shadow and Evil in Fairytales*, Dallas, Spring Publications, 1974, p. 120.
2. M. Esther Harding, *The 'I' and 'Not-I'*, Princeton, Princeton University Press, 1965.
3. Alice Miller, *The Drama of the Gifted Child*, trans. Ruth Ward, New York, Basic Books, 1981.

7 Four People on a Spiritual Journey

1. C. G. Jung, *Memories, Dreams and Reflections*, New York, Vintage Books, 1963.
2. Lawrence Durrell, *A Spirit of Place*, BBC program on Greece.

8 Chad: an Analysis with Poems as Markers

1. Marie-Louise von Franz *et al.* with C. G. Jung, *Man and his Symbols*, New York, Doubleday, 1965.
2. Michael Fordham, 'Jungian Views of the Body–Mind Relationship', *Spring*, 1974, pp. 166–78.

9 Antoine: the Spirit in the Body

1. C. A. Meier, *Soul and Body: Essays on the Theories of C. G. Jung*, Santa Monica, The Lapis Press, 1986, p. 238.
2. Jung, *Memories, Dreams and Reflections*, p. 318.

3. Robin Lane Fox, *Pagans and Christians*, New York, Harper & Row/London, Viking, 1986, pp. 162, 163.
4. Joseph Campbell, *The Inner Reaches of Outer Space*, New York, Alfred Van der Marck Edition, 1986, p. 11.
5. C. G. Jung, *Mysterium Coniunctionis, Collected Works*, Vol. 14, pp. 465, 466.
6. Arnold Mindell, *Working with the Dreaming Body*, London and Boston, Routledge & Kegan Paul, 1985, pp. 85–92.
7. Barbara Hannah, *Jung: His Life and Work*, London, Michael Joseph, 1977, p. 313.
8. Cf. Mindell, *The Dreambody in Relationships*, for specific procedures for processing the material of the relationship channel of information.

10 Conclusion

1. Arnold Mindell, *Dreambody: The Body's Role in Revealing the Self*, Santa Monica, Sigo Press, 1982.
2. James Hillman, *Re-Visioning Psychology*, New York, Harper & Row, 1975.
3. William Windelband, *A History of Philosophy*, Vol. II, New York, Harper & Brothers, 1958.
4. Emma Jung, *Animus and Anima*, New York, The Analytical Psychology Club of New York, 1957, p. 54.
5. ibid., p. 45.
6. *Dreambody*, p. 84.
7. ibid.
8. Hugh Downs, *Rhythms of a Himalayan Village*, New York, Harper & Row, 1980.

Bibliography

Ashton-Warner, Sylvia, *Teacher*, New York, Bantam Publishers, 1971.

Buber, Martin, *Eclipse of God*, Westport, Conn., Greenwood Press, 1977.

   I and Thou, New York, Charles Scribner's Sons, second edition, 1958.

Campbell, Joseph, *The Inner Reaches of Outer Space*, New York, Alfred Van der Marck Edition, 1986.

Downs, Hugh, *Rhythms of a Himalayan Village*, New York, Harper & Row, 1980.

Durrell, Lawrence, *A Spirit of Place*, BBC program on Greece.

Fordham, Michael, 'Jungian Views of the Body–Mind Relationship', *Spring*, 1974, pp. 166–78.

Fowles, John, *The French Lieutenant's Woman*, London, Pan, 1987.

Fox, Robin Lane, *Pagans and Christians*, New York, Harper & Row/London, Viking, 1986.

Franz, Marie-Louise von, *Shadow and Evil in Fairytales*, Dallas, Spring Publications, 1974.

Hannah, Barbara, *Jung: His Life and Work*, London, Michael Joseph, 1977.

Harding, M. Esther. *The 'I' and 'Not-I'*, Princeton, Princeton University Press, 1965.

   Psychic Energy: Its Source and Its Transformation, Washington, DC, The Bollingen Foundation, second edition, 1963.

Hillman, James, *Re-Visioning Psychology*, New York, Harper & Row, 1975.

Jung, C. G. (with M.-L. von Franz, Joseph L. Henderson, Jolande Jacobi, Aniela Jaffe), *Man and His Symbols*, New York, Doubleday, 1965.

   The Collected Works of C. G. Jung, eds. Sir Herbert Read, Michael Fordham and Gerhard Adler, trans. R. F. C. Hull (except for Vol. 2), Princeton, Princeton University Press (Bollingen Series XX)/London, Routledge & Kegan Paul, 1953–. Volumes cited in this publication: Vol. 8, *The Structure and Dynamics of the Psyche*, 1960; Vol. 9, *Psychology and Religion*, 1963; Vol. 13, *Alchemical Studies*, 1967; Vol. 14, *Mysterium Coniunctionis*.

Memories, Dreams, Reflections, New York, Vintage Books, 1963.

Jung, Emma, *Animus and Anima*, New York, The Analytical Psychology Club of New York, 1957, p. 54.

Meier, C. A., *Soul and Body: Essays on the Theories of C. G. Jung*, Santa Monica, The Lapis Press, 1986.

Michlem, Neil, 'The Intolerable Image: the Mythic Background of Psychosis', *Spring*, 1979, p. 16.

'On Hysteria: the Mythical Syndrome', *Spring*, 1974, p. 155.

Miller, Alice, *The Drama of the Gifted Child*, trans. Ruth Ward, New York, Basic Books, 1981.

Mindell, Arnold, *City Shadows: Psychological Interventions in Psychiatry*, London and New York, Routledge & Kegan Paul, 1988.

The Dreambody in Relationships, London and Boston, Routledge & Kegan Paul, 1987/Arkana, 1988.

Dreambody: The Body's Role in Revealing the Self, Santa Monica, Sigo Press, 1982.

River's Way: The Process Science of the Dreambody, London and Boston, Routledge & Kegan Paul, 1985.

Working with the Dreaming Body, London and Boston, Routledge & Kegan Paul, 1985.

Pautler, T. G., 'Parkinson's Disease, Immobility and the Repression of Psychosis' (mimeo.), 1985.

Tulku, Tarthang, *Skillful Means*, Berkeley, Dharma Publishing, 1978.

Windelband, William, *A History of Philosophy*, Vol. II, New York, Harper & Brothers, 1958.